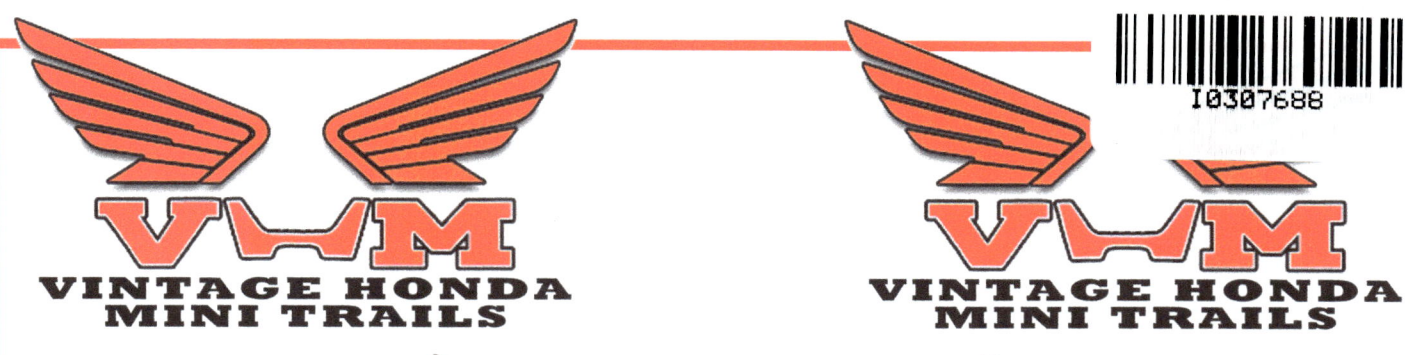

PARTS  SERVICE

• COMPLETE MOTORCYCLES •

We have been collecting, buying, and selling vintage Honda Motorcycles for about 35 years, specializing in:

Honda MR50, QA50, Z50A, Z50M, Z50Z, CL70, CT70, CT70H, SL70, XL70, XR75, SL90, SL90K, and ST90.

We stock most parts NOS or Used for most of the models listed.

We have over 8,000 part numbers for the NOS parts and we ship Worldwide!

Check out the parts and bikes on our website:
www.vintagehondaminitrails.com

Email us through the website,
or call us: 810-797-5507

We're open 24 hours a day, 7 days a week, 365 days a year (even holidays).

Honda Mini Trail Enthusiast's Guide
All Z50, 1968 - 1999, 49cc

by Jeremy Polson

Published by:
Wolfgang Publications, Inc.
P.O. Box 223
Stillwater, MN 55082

LEGALS

First published in 2016 by Wolfgang Publications Inc.
P.O. Box 223, Stillwater, MN 55082

© Jeremy Polson, 2016

All rights reserved. With the exception of quoting brief passages for the purposes of review, no part of this publication may be reproduced without prior written permission from the publisher.

The information in this book is true and complete to the best of our knowledge. All recommendations are made without any guarantee on the part of the author or publisher, who also disclaim any liability incurred in connection with the use of this data or specific details.

We recognize that some words, model names and designations, for example, mentioned herein are the property of the trademark holder. We use them for identification purposes only. This is not an official publication.

ISBN   978-1-941064-32-0
Printed and bound in the U.S.A.

"You meet the nicest people on a Honda"

Acknowledgements

Not only do I love the Z50 Mini Trail but I always enjoy talking with people that are just as crazy, well almost as crazy as I am about everything in the Z50 world.

There are many people that I would like to thank for making this book possible as well as for helping me out in the collector Mini Trail hobby.

My brother Chad Polson-my partner in crime, he has an eye for quality parts and always seems to find that rare Mini Trail or part.

My grandpa Ron Polson for teaching me how to buy, sell, and negotiate. This passion rubbed off onto my brother and me and there isn't a time that we get together that we are not talking about something with an engine.

My uncle Bill Polson-he helped us acquire our first Mini Trail and gave me the lead on finding my high serial number saddleback '68.

My grandpa Harlan Behn, his truck has hauled more Mini Trails then we can even remember.

My friend Chris Langdon for being a major help in the restorations I did over an 8 year period. Chris shuttled parts and restored bikes across the country countless times and has continued to play a part in this wonderful hobby.

Ron Demianiuk for doing the photo shoots helping make this book possible.

I would also like to thank some of the great people that I have met over the years that have helped me out with my personal collection as well as making this book possible by providing pictures as well as documentation and information.

Jerry Ure Jr. of Michigan: Jerry has provided pictures, information, and parts, and service. Jerry has painted countless frames for me and reproduced endless decals off of originals I have provided. When I need a part whether common or rare he seems to be able to come up with it.

Tim Lavoi of Minnesota: Tim has done engine restorations for my clients for over a decade and he does the best work on the planet hands down!

Ron Chiluk of Illinois: Ron is the master of carburetor restorations as well as brake plate and wheel hub restoration. Nobody has the knowledge and expertise for making old beat up parts look like the way they did when they left the Honda factory over 40 years ago like Ron.

Jan Jarde of California: Jan led me to Astro Plating for chrome restoration services as well as for information on Mini Trail and Monkey bike history.

The staff at Northeast Vintage Cycle provided pictures as well as many rare NOS parts over the years and continued service of new OEM parts for my client's restorations.

Pete Klein of Iowa: Pete provided pictures and information on 1968 Z50A's.

Ken Peare of New Jersey, Ryan Hoffman of Canada, Todd Thorson of Iowa, Gregg Davidian, of New Jersey, Randy Ess of Oregon, Cameron Johnson of Washington, Rod Fukuma of Washington, Scott Leach of California, and Jason Bruce of Florida: All of these Mini Trail enthusiasts have played an important part in this book by providing pictures, documentation, and information.

Mark Mitchell of California: Mark has provided information, pictures, documentation, and most importantly I cannot thank him enough for selling me 3 of the worlds rarest Z50A's.

I would most like to thank Gary Lewis of Michigan, owner of Vintage Honda Mini Trails. Gary has been in the Mini Trail business for over 34 years and has a wealth of knowledge, hundreds of original motorcycles; quality used parts, documentation, and one of the largest collections of NOS Mini Trail Z50 parts in the world. Gary has been a huge help in making this book possible.

• • • • •

If you have a nice all original Z50 that you are interested in selling or if you are interested in contacting Jeremy about anything Mini Trail related he can be reached at jpolsonz50@gmail.com

Honda Mini Trail Enthusiast's Guide – 1968-1999

Table of Contents

Preface - Dedication - Credits
Background 6

In The Beginning
The Mini Bike Craze 8

The First Mini Trail
1966-67 Z50M 10

Chapter 1
The Birth of the Mini 14

Chapter 2
1969-1970 Z50 K1 45

Chapter 3
1970-1971 Z50 K2 59

Chapter 4
1972 Z50A K3 71

Chapter 5
1973 Z50A K4 77

Chapter 6
1974 Z50A K5 80

Chapter 7
1975 Z50A K6 83

Chapter 8
1976 Z50A 86

Chapter 9
1977 Z50A 89

Chapter 10
1978 Z50A 92

Chapter 11
1979 Z50R 94

Chapter 12
1980 Z50R 97

Chapter 13
1981 Z50R 100

Chapter 14
1982 Z50R 102

Chapter 15
1983 Z50R 104

Chapter 16
1984 Z50R 105

Chapter 17
1985 Z50R 107

Chapter 18
1986 Z50R 110

Chapter 19
1986 Z50RD 112

Chapter 20
1987 Z50R 117

Chapter 21
1988 Z50R 120

Chapter 22
1989 Z50R 122

Chapter 23
1991 Z50R 125

Chapter 24
1992 Z50R 128

Chapter 25
1993 Z50R 130

Chapter 26
1994 Z50R 132

Chapter 27
1995 Z50R 134

Chapter 28
1996 Z50R 136

Chapter 29
1997 Z50R 138

Chapter 30
1998 Z50R 140

Chapter 31
1999 Z50R 142

Preface

Everyone remembers their first mini bike or if you were fortunate enough, your first Mini Trail. If you didn't have one, chances are you wanted one as a child. Pedal bikes were cool, but there was just something special about having an engine and the ability to climb hills and go fast that grabbed kids' attention.

My love affair with the Mini Trail began in 1987 in the fourth grade. There was a Honda CT70 K0 for sale in the Duluth News Tribune where I grew up that caught my dad's eye. They were asking $110.00 for it. My dad called on it being that he had one along with a Z50 as a kid and was curious about it. My mom was against me and my brother getting a mini bike. Little did she know I was dead set on getting a mini bike.

Finally, in the summer of 1991 after mowing the lawn at my uncle's house, his neighbor Fred showed up on a Z50 K1. After one ride I fell in love with it. I didn't care what shape it was in, it ran and I had to have it. Fred went home and much to our surprise he let us have the Z50.

It wasn't but a month later and we finally saw another ad for a CT70 in the paper. The Z50 was great but I wanted a CT70. We called on it and it was still available. We went and picked it up the next morning for $325.00. It was a 1975 Mighty Green CT70. I still have the CT70.

Now that I had a nice Honda CT70 my brother wanted to get a nice Z50. He ended up getting a

Z50A K2 that didn't run. The plan was to put the best parts together to make one bike and that is what we did.

In the mid 1990's, my brother had a local body shop do a paint job restoration on the Z50A K2. After seeing his restoration, I had to find a Z50A to restore. I was 16 years old at the time and was driving a 1967 Camaro, a car that most adults would lust over. I am not sure what it is to this day but I can go to a car show and if I see a Mini Trail it completely consumes me and I lose all interest in the cars at the show. The hunt was on again!

In 1996 my dad was given a phone number of a guy that had a 1964 Nova that we were supposed to go and look at for my brother. When we showed up to look at the car the guy wasn't set on a price or even sure if he wanted to sell it. In the back corner of his garage he had a nice all original candy red/silver Z50A K1. He said the Z50 belonged to his son, and it wasn't for sale.

To make a long story short we waited an entire year and were hoping to go back and purchase the Z50 again and were not really interested in the Nova because we didn't think it was for sale either. Much to our surprise the Nova was for sale but the Z50 still wasn't.

We got really excited because my brother really wanted to get a classic car and so we went home and told my dad about the Nova. We purchased the Nova and left a $410.00 offer on the table for the Z50. About a week later the son called and said the Z50 was for sale. I purchased the Z50 and it wasn't but a couple years later and they really started to climb in price on the internet. My brother and I started hunting harder and harder for CT70's and Z50's and as the old saying goes, "the rest is history".

Over the past 27 years I have owned several hundred Mini Trails, sold thousands of parts, restored numerous show quality examples for clients, and continue to buy-sell-& trade on a weekly basis. Many people have come and gone in this hobby over the years but it seems to me that every year I get a little deeper into it. I am always in search of the Holy Grail to speak of when it comes to finding a rare original low hour Mini Trail and that is what keeps me going.

I wasn't born when the Mini Trail first made its way into Honda dealers in the late 1960's. It's the baby boomers like my dad and uncle that will look upon these pages and remember how much they enjoyed these bikes as kids. It's also all those kids that didn't have their wish come true of owning a Z50 when they were young. But often times they are the ones that get into them later in life and they are the ones that have helped the hobby grow. It is also for the younger generations that are starting to appreciate vintage motorcycles and are looking to get educated and take on this wonderful hobby. Whatever your connection was and is today, you are the collectors. You have a passion for collector motorcycles and a love for the Honda Mini Trail. This book goes out to all of you.

- Jeremy Polson

Dedication

I would like to dedicate this book to my parents Rod and Sandy Polson. My mom got me interested in collecting at a very young age and my dad introduced me to the Honda Z50 over 25 years ago. The countless hours spent searching for parts, working on Mini Trails, and maintaining the ones my brother and I currently own are memories that will last a lifetime.

Credits:
p.70 (Cameron Johnson Collection)
p.79 (Cameron Johnson Collection)
p.93 (Ken Peare Collection)
p.104 (Ryan Hoffman Collection)
p.106 (Ryan Hoffman Collection)
p.109 (Ryan Hoffman Collection)
p.110 (Jeremy Polson Collection)
p.116 (Ryan Hoffman Collection)
p.119 (Ryan Hoffman Collection)
p.121 (Ryan Hoffman Collection)
p.124 (Ryan Hoffman Collection)
p.129 (Photo by Shane Burke Studios, Jason Bruce Collection)
p.131 (Ken Peare Collection)
p.133 (Gregg Davidian Collection)
p.135 (Gregg Davidian Collection)
p.137 (Gregg Davidian Collection)
p.141 (Chad Polson Collection)

In the Beginning

The Mini Bike Craze – How it all began

Introduction

After restoring several bikes, analyzing original bikes, and looking at bikes others have restored I became fascinated with trying to figure out what parts actually came on particular bikes from the factory. After further investigations I started to realize that there were many variations in particular parts just within one production year. It was at this point that I gave up on restoring Mini Trails for myself. I sold off all my restored Mini Trails and started hunting for original bikes in low hour unrestored condition. I enjoy restoring bikes and helping others find parts, but my passion is collecting original UN-restored bikes. As the old saying goes, "you can always restore them, but they are only original once".

The purpose of this book is to cover the Z50A as well as the Z50R from 1968 until the end of production in 1999. This book is not intended to go into detail on the Monkey bike, but rather just give a brief overview of the early models to show how the Z50A came to be.

All of the information in this book is based on hands on experience working with original Mini Trails as well as talking with fellow Mini Trail enthusiasts that have had similar experiences wrenching on original bikes over the years. I have provided the Honda recommendations for frame and engine serial numbers as a guide to let you know where Honda supposedly made the parts

Above: Restored example of a Z100. This model was never available as a production motorcycle.

Above: 1961 Z100 at the Honda Collection Hall in Japan. Restored Z100.

Left Center: 1963 white tank Z100. They also came with red tanks.

Above: Promotional calendar photo of the Tama Tech Amusement Park Ride in Japan- Gary Lewis Collection.

Right Center: 1964 CZ100

Left Bottom: 1965 CZ100

Above: Z100 that original & current owner Steve Simon received from his father. It is 1 of 3 that Honda brought over to vote on at a dealer meeting. The other 2 went back to Japan.

Right Bottom: 1966 CZ100

changes during production. As you may have experienced, it is evident that these production figures are not always accurate.

Let the pictures, the engine numbers, the frame numbers, the literature, documentation, and my explanations help unravel the Mini Trail mystery. More importantly let this be a starting point as I know there is much more to be discovered. It is my hope that this book will generate a lot of interest, get people talking, hopefully unearth some rare motorcycles, and most importantly move the hobby to the next level.

The Early Days

Gear heads started building home-made mini bikes in the 1930s - bicycle frames fitted with engines. In the 1950s drag racers and motor heads built mini bikes as pit bikes for driving around the pits. Eventually the "mini bike" fad caught on and kids began riding them. By the mid to late sixties numerous companies began to produce mini bikes. Campgrounds and dirt tracks were overcome with mini bikes; they were a nation-wide craze.

Honda as a company started building production motorcycles in the 1950s. It wouldn't be too many years into production before they jumped on the mini bike bandwagon and produced the first mini bike, the Z100 Monkey bike.

The Z100 was more or less a prototype, being that it was not actually for sale to the public. Production numbers on the Z100 are sketchy, but it is rumored that up to a dozen or so of the first model were produced. The story of the Monkey Bike began in 1961 with the Z100, as an attraction at Tama Tech Park, a Honda-owned motorsports theme park, at Honda's Suzuki Circuit in Japan.

The Z100 had a long white fuel tank, a small bright red frame, wide but small 5-inch wheels, powered by a C100 engine from a Super Cub with a semi-automatic transmission.

Most people don't know that the 1961 Z100 was imported into the USA until they were all recalled and sent back to Japan due to broken frames. The units used at Tama Tech with headlamps and taillights were the recalled US rejects, as the ones built specifically for Tama Tech weren't built with lighting of any kind.

The Z100 proved to be popular with park visitors. Honda needed something for the kids to play on and enjoy at the park and the Z100 was their answer. The term "kid" took on a whole new meaning when adults fell in love with the new creation just like the kids did.

With its compact dimensions, Z100 adult riders were described as looking like Monkeys, hence the term "Monkey Bike." It probably didn't take a genius to figure out that the latest creation was an instant success. Honda knew what direction they needed to head, the reaction at the Tama Tech Park paved the way, and as the old saying goes, the rest is history. There is a pristine example of a fully restored Z100 on display in Japan at the Honda Collection Hall Museum.

Is the Z100 the most valuable and rarest Mini Trail of all? Continue reading to find out!

The CZ100 Takes Production; Honda Officially Enters The Mini Bike World

The first production Honda Monkey Bike came out in 1963 when Honda produced the CZ100, a Monkey bike similar to the Z100. Honda first produced the Mark 1 series 1 CZ100. It had a white tank, a rigid red frame, 5 inch street tires, a small black vinyl one person seat, a long front fender, no speedometer, no serial number stamped into the frame, and a C100 engine. As of today it is rumored that there are only 7 known to exist in the world.

In January of 2014 a restored example sold at a Las Vegas motorcycle auction. This particular model was found attached to an amusement park ride in England before undergoing a full restoration.

The Mark 2 Series 1 CZ100 looked almost identical to the series 1 model other than the tank matched the frame, both were painted red. According to Jan Harde at Monkeybike.com, around 89 Mark 2 series 1s were produced.

Honda continued to produce the CZ100 until 1966. Subtle changes occurred from the introduction in 1963 until the final CZ100 rolled off the assembly line. The CZ100 has gained in popularity in the United States over the last several years because of the internet. Being that it was not sold in the United States many collectors have started to obtain them from foreign collectors.

The Z100 and the CZ100 paved the way for the next model, the Z50M.

The First Mini Trail

1966 - 67 Z50M

In 1966 a new model emerged, the Z50M. The Z50M is the bike that paved the way for the American mini bike we know as the Z50A, or simply the "Mini Trail 50". This model sported a red frame, chain guard, taillight bracket with tool kit holder, and air box. Just like the Z100 and the CZ100, the Z50M lacked any suspension components in the rear of the unit, or in the front forks like most motorcycles.

All early models featured a welded neck white fuel tank with round Honda wing badges. The fuel tanks had a thin butterfly on/off gas cap. However, Jerry Ure Jr. owns an original Z50M tank that still sports the factory red paint. How many red tank models were made? It remains a mystery. Off white molded plastic fenders helped keep the mud and water off the rider. All versions of the M came with an on/off frame-mounted key switch under the tank and a front-fork mounted horn.

English Z50M with small headlight and low swept Exhaust-Jeremy Polson Collection.

A chrome foot brake pedal took care of the rear braking and on the opposite side of the mini bike was an up/down style shifter in chrome. A rather thinly padded long foldable plaid or Tartan style seat kept the rider comfortable.

The handlebars were collapsible and could be folded down by loosening two black plastic knobs to make the Z50M compact enough to stow away easily in a car, boat, airplane, travel trailer, or wherever the owner needed to save space.

Only one hand brake lever was found on the M and it was a front brake cable that mounted on the right hand bar and attached to the hi/low control switch. The left handle bar had no holes or a lever perch. The headlight bucket on all three versions of the M came with a speedometer. The Japanese Domestic and French models came with a speedometer in Km/h and the English version came in miles per hour. The 49cc engine was paired with a three-speed transmission with an automatic clutch.

The Z50M was produced in three distinctive models for three markets. The general export /English model had a small headlight and a low style muffler. The Japanese domestic model and the most common version had a small style headlight and a triangular shaped muffler up behind the engine and placed under the seat. Enthusiasts refer to this as the lunch box style muffler. The final version is the French

Top picture: (Japanese Domestic Z50M with "lunch box" style Muffler-Pete Klein Collection

French Z50M with large style headlight and low swept Exhaust-Jerry Ure Jr. Collection

11

model. It has a large headlight, which is the most distinctive feature and makes the bike highly sought after. It has a hi/lo switch for the headlight, and like the English version it to had the low style muffler.

Additional Z50M Information:

Of the three versions, the French model is among the rarest of them all. Like many early Honda motorcycles, production numbers are

Original "HM" stamped right side bar mounted Honda mirror.
Under seat Scarlet Red round canister tool box.

sketchy, but it is believed that up to 100 or so of these French models were produced. Jerry Ure Jr. of Michigan has owned a couple of them and has had no problem selling them to collectors around the world.

Long time Mini Trail enthusiast Mark Mitchell of California really enjoys the Z50M model and enlightened me on a rare German version of the Z50M. What makes a German model so rare? In Germany only a few models were sold. By Special TUV road regulations, the production version of the Z50M was not approved for the German road traffic. A few Honda importers modified their bikes so they could be used on German roads. Either way, the German model Z50M was sold in such small quantities that they are very sought after by collectors today.

In all of my years of collecting I personally never wanted a Z50M. That is until January of 2016 when fellow Mini Trail collector Ryan Hoffman of Edmonton Canada sent me a text that said, "interested in a Z50M?" My first response was no, but then I quickly texted back and said, "if it is an all-original bike I might be, get me pictures."

After about two months of going back and forth with his client I finally struck a deal on the bike. The hinge point was not the price; it was whether or not the client actually wanted to sell it. I just remained patient waiting to find out if I would be adding a Z50M to my collection. I actually went back and forth in my mind in the mean time because I wasn't entirely sure I wanted it either. Once the deal was reached the next plan was to get it to the United States. And that isn't an easy task at the Canadian border. That is unless you ship the entire bike in parts and reassemble. Around April of 2016 the entire bike had finally arrived and was assembled and ready to be photographed for the book a few months later.

The 5 inch tires and the Tartan seat really are something to admire when you have one in your possession. They certainly are the type of bike that once you see them up close and in person I am convinced that you will want to own one!

English model with a low swept exhaust, also used on the French model.

Z50M collapsible Tartan plaid seat

Early acrylic/plastic tank emblems

Chapter 1

1968 Honda Z50A: The Birth of the Mini

Engine serial number beginning and ending: Z50AE 100001~120087
Frame number beginning and ending: Z50A 1000001~120087

All of a sudden mini bikes are respectable. In the past they have been looked upon as a stepchild of the cycle industry but one swift, bold stroke changed all that. What type of incident changed the situation? Only the biggest name in the motorcycle business can bring something like this off and that's just what happened. Honda is now selling a mini bike. The 50cc Mini Trail is its name and fun is its game.

Cycle Guide Magazine-January 1969

In September of 1968, Honda started selling its first Mini Trail built for American consumers. Production ran until March of 1969 and a total of 20,087 Mini Trails were produced in the first model year. The production name for this model is the Honda Z50A. The Z50 K0 name did not come into use until later years when people started referring to it by that name. It was referred to by that name in the 1980's Honda I.D. guide book. Later, Honda sales brochures make note that "K"

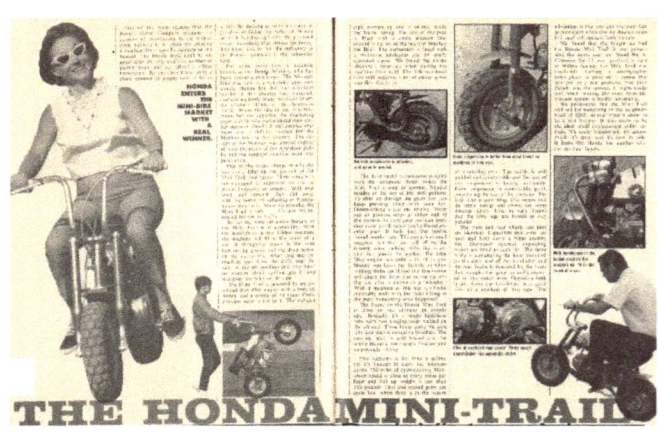

means model change, thus the reason the first model does not have a "K" behind its name. The 1969 Z50A is referred to as a K1.

The primitive little mini bike came without a headlight or taillight; it had an on/off toggle switch, and was intended for off-road use only. The Z50A came in just two color combinations; scarlet red and ivory white and bright yellow and ivory White. All models came with ivory white hand grips and front and rear ivory white plastic hand brake levers. They were trimmed out in cloud silver painted front and rear fenders and wheels mounted on 3.50x8 inch knobby tires. The engine was a 49cc, with a 3-speed automatic transmission.

According to the May of 1969 issue of Mini Bike Guide Magazine, Honda produced 3,000 Mini Trail Z50's in the first batch of production. When all of them sold out by December of 1968, Dealers began begging for more. What's interesting about this figure is that a fellow by the name of Jack Ortiz purchased a bright yellow/ivory white Z50A on November 29th, 1968 from Norm Reeves Honda in California and it was frame number 104332 with engine number 104443. This Mini Trail is currently in my personal collection (see bill of sale).

On November 21st of 1968 Cappy's Sales & Service of New Jersey received a manufacturer's statement of origin for Z50A frame number 104176. Fred Siegel purchased this particular bike on December 6th. It is currently owned by Ken Peare of New Jersey. On December 2nd, 1968 C. White of Tucson Arizona purchased a brand new Z50A. The frame serial number is 105067.

These three pieces of documentation prove that over 5,000 Mini Trails were produced and sold by early December. Well over 2,000 more than was said to have been produced.

One of the greatest mysteries in the Mini Trail world is to figure out what all of the differences are between parts and model changes on the 1968 Honda Z50A. Perhaps an even bigger mystery is to figure out which bikes came with which parts and when the changes took place during production.

When trying to figure out all of the changes it is important to note that not all parts changes were considered new parts, but rather just

Paul Ellingson Jr. Christmas 1968 with his new Z50A-still owns it

Cycle World article featuring a Tall Bar with an elusive 6 seam seat.

New Old Stock boxes of NGK & ND spark Plugs-Jeremy Polson Collection

variations of the same part. Some parts changed two, three, or more times during the production run and were not listed as different parts in the catalog or microfiche, but rather were considered the same part with the same part number. It is also important to note that like many Honda motorcycles over the years, not all parts came from the same vendor, thus making two bikes coming down the assembly line not necessarily identical. The multiple vendor situations helps explain many of the mysteries as to why some mini bikes had parts that people call "early" and parts some call "later" parts when in fact that is not necessarily the case. True, there are some parts that were never found on the later model Z50As but to say all the early bikes had certain parts or features has proven to be false. In fact, some later serial number bikes have parts that disprove this fact.

A prototype motorcycle:

It is important to keep in mind that an item built during the first year of production often times undergoes many changes during that year to make the product better, safer, or easier to produce. The 1968 Z50A was basically a prototype motorcycle. During production many parts were changed for various reasons. Some parts were changed for safety reasons while others were changed because of design weaknesses or simply because the new part was quicker and easier to produce.

For whatever reason a part was changed during production, it makes the '68 Z50A one of the most talked about Mini Trails and certainly one of the most desired by collectors.

The big questions among collectors are: what are all of the parts changes made during the production run? And what parts are correct for the early, middle, and end of the run Mini Trails? The only true answer is; the way it came from the factory. Simply put, Honda Mini Trails were built on an assembly line, and most importantly, built to ride. Special care and attention to detail was the farthest thing from the factory workers' minds when assembling the bikes. Unlike the classic car world, matching numbers is not something that was considered when the bikes were being put together. In fact, it is not uncommon to see frame and engine serial numbers off by several hundred, or even several thousand.

Again, mix in the fact that parts came from different vendors and often times new parts were brought into the factory and put on the front of parts racks thus pushing the earlier production parts to the back of the rack instead of using them up. It was also common practice to have some parts pulled for quality control inspections and later put back on the parts racks to be used later.

On more than one occasion Mini Trails left the factory with non-matching tires as well as engines left over from the previous model year. I own, and have owned, several Mini Trails with worn parts that have another factory paint color underneath the top coat of paint.

What is a Slant Guard?

Often times the 1968 Honda Z50A is referred to as a "slant guard". So what is a slant guard? The name Slant guard refers to the muffler protector that is mounted on a slant on the kicker/muffler side of the Mini Trail. Rumor has it that this was a design flaw or mistake. It was also rumored that the exposed pipe resulted in a number of leg burns thus causing Honda to make a change to the way the muffler protector mounts to the frame. True or not, Honda Produced 5,306 Mini Trails from frame number 100001 to frame number 105306 before switching the frame and muffler protector.

According to the Honda parts catalog and microfiche, all frame serial numbers at 105306 or below required the 18360-045-670C (Scarlet Red), 18360-045-670 XB (Bright Yellow) or 18360-045-670Z (Base Coating) muffler protector.

The Honda parts catalog and microfiche show the muffler guard protector problem being switched to the longer muffler guard at frame number 105307. The new design scheme; the straight muffler protector carried on through to the end of the '68 production and was used on the K1 and K2 models.

Later model '68 Z50As are referred to as "straight guards" because they were fitted with the corrected straight muffler protector. The highest slant guard frame number that I have seen is serial number 105303 and it is a red/white example. I have never seen a frame serial number above 105306 with a slant muffler guard. If anyone has

Scarlet Red Slant guard muffler protector, 1st 5,306 Z50A's

Bright Yellow Slant guard muffler protector

Tall Bar 100797 previously owned by my brother Chad, sold to Rod Fukuma of Washington. N.O.S. tall bars, perfect original seat, and N.O.S Nitto tires compliment the rest of the hard to find new old stock parts making this a TRUE 100-point restoration.

Tall Bar serial number 100217 with engine 100334, currently owned by Mark Mitchell of California. The lowest serial number yellow tall bar known to exist.

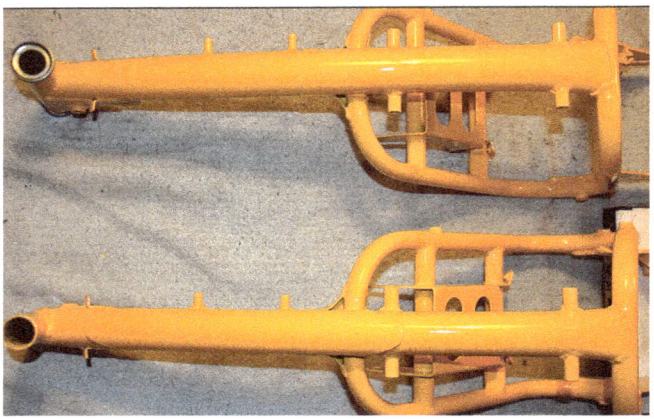

Top frame has the standard thick backbone. The bottom frame has the extra gusset plate welded to the backbone for extra support, bottom frame is known as a "Saddleback".

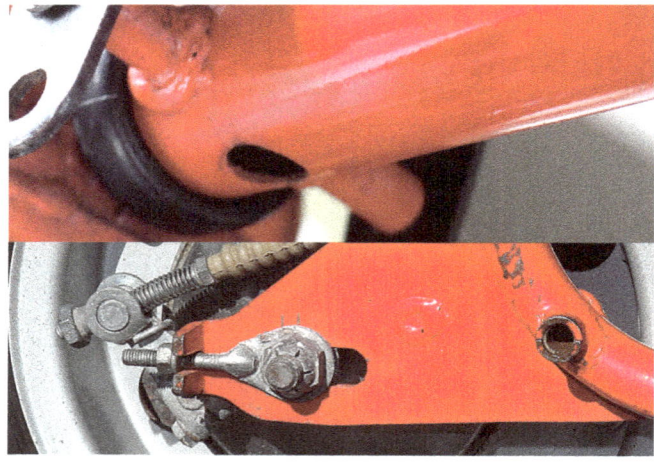

Upper: Saddle back frames have two water port holes on the bottom of the back bone. Lower: All '68s and early K1s have 4 hash marks in the frame for chain adjustments, later frames have five.

one, please come forward!

The most confusing and misleading information over the years for me is when people say, "all of the early bikes had this part or that part, or this is a tall bar part or slant guard part, or all of the early serial number Mini Trails were Scarlet Red/Ivory white." It is statements like those that added fuel to my fire to want to write this book. I will explain what I have experienced over the years using a variety of examples with pictures of original '68s over a wide range of frame and engine serial numbers. As the old saying goes, "the proof is in the pudding." The easiest way to talk about the changes is to break the Mini Trail down part by part and explain them with pictures of actual Mini Trails, engine numbers, frame serial numbers, and printed media. With that being said, let the journey begin!

The Frame

Let's start with the frame, being that we have already established what a slant guard is. This topic is one of my favorites and it is my hope that my findings will bring even the most knowledgeable Mini Trail enthusiasts to their knees and throw many theories out the window.

Now that we have established what a slant guard is and what the Honda recommendations are for frame serial numbers let's dig a little deeper. Where it gets tricky is that some of the Slant guards had a smaller diameter backbone or what enthusiasts call a "saddle back" because an extra gusset plate was welded to the top of the frame under the tank for extra support. Exactly how many were made with the smaller backbone and gusset plate remains a mystery.

However, I have gathered a range of serial numbers to try and piece the puzzle together. Randy Ess of Oregon owns 14 Slant guards, all of which lack the "saddle back" top gusset support plate. His Slant guard frame numbers are the following: 101625, 101962, 101929, 102015, 102562, 102803, 102809, 103043, 103062, 103314, 103619, 103700, 104553, 104725, and 104906.

Jerry Ure Jr. of Battle Creek Michigan owns two high serial number Slant guard frames. He has serial numbers 105205 and 105266. Both of which are non-saddleback frames.

I do know for a fact that the following frames have the "saddle back": 100070, 100128, 100217, 100503, 100609, 100645, 100659, 100720, 100797, 100799, 100896, 100923, 100965, 100992,100996, and 101016.

As of June of 2014, I sold a non-saddleback frame with serial number 101153 with engine number 101575. Frame number 101577 in original red paint lacks the saddle back as does an original yellow frame with serial number 101727.

With the following examples and some logical reasoning one might conclude that all frames around 101149 or so and below had the saddle back frame and all frames at or above 101150 did not have the saddle back. Sounds logical right? Here is where it gets tricky.

Frame number 101213 surfaced and it has a saddle back and when frame number 101037 surfaced in original red paint with one bent up tall bar I was shocked to find out that it did not have a saddle back on the frame. Frame number 101213 is just one frame slightly above the others but still early enough to maybe have been pulled by the R&D department and put back in the pile to be stamped is what one might think. But then how does one explain why frame number 101037 does not have a saddle back? Just when you think you have a solid frame range established that is when you need to keep hunting for more evidence because the second you think you have things figured out that is when it gets interesting. Think you have it figured out? Hang onto to your saddles, it gets even trickier!

Out of all of the Slant guards I own and have owned, I had two that are 55 frame serial numbers apart. I sold one of them to Rod Fukuma of Washington and it is a slant guard with frame number 102992 and engine 103060. What is so interesting about it is that it HAS a thick backbone like the K1 and K2s. Based on the above information, it should right?

Well, based on that frame serial number and the above information one might conclude that there certainly were no "saddle back" frames beyond 102992. The most interesting fact is that I have frame number 103147 with engine number

The lowest frame and engine numbers known to exist. The Frame is owned by Scott Leach of California and the engine is owned by Randy Ess of Oregon.

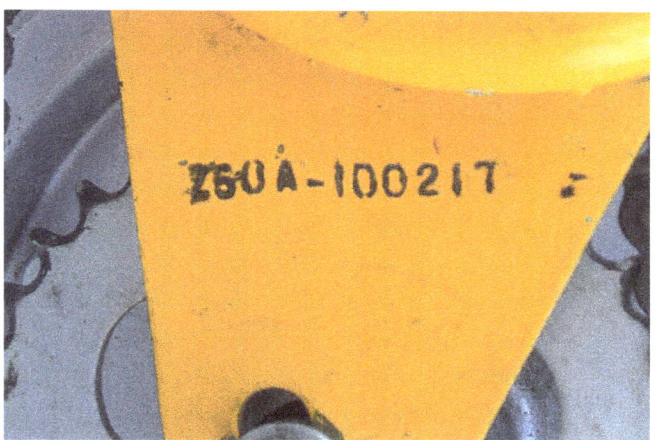
Earliest yellow Tall Bar frame serial number known to exist-Mark Mitchell collection.

Scarlet Red Tall Bar Saddleback- Jeremy Polson collection.

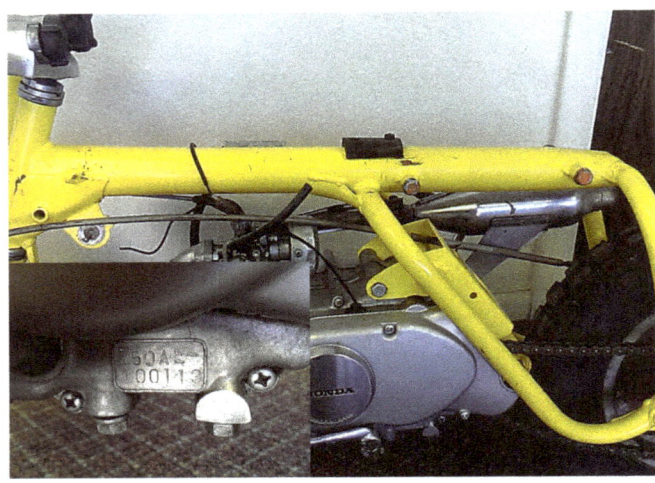

Frame number 103110 with engine number 100113 owned by "Big Daddy" Ric Ramsey of Utah.

Frame number 3149 with engine serial number 100114, Jesse Buckley Collection.

Frame number 103147 with engine number 100115, Jeremy Polson Collection.

100115 and it HAS the narrow backbone with the extra gusset plate. Both Mini Trails were purchased from the original owners and both were in original paint when I purchased them. The Scarlet red/Ivory white Mini Trail with the saddle back frame is still in original paint.

After talking with many Mini Trail enthusiasts about my "saddle back" frame with the low engine serial number a few theories have been discussed. The first theory is that it could be a mis-stamped frame. Some enthusiasts feel that the frame should have been stamped number 100147. If that were the case it would be closer to the engine number which again is 100115.

Another theory is that the frame was built early and possibly pulled by the research and development department or the quality control department and later stamped, painted and put back into production. The main reason why some feel this theory is not as likely is because the engine and frame are over 3,000 numbers apart and as far as '68 production numbers go that is very unusual. Or is it?

After owning frame number 103147 with engine number 100115 for over 14 years many theories have crossed my mind and it has always remained a mystery as to why they are so far apart. There are certainly people out there that think that the engine did not come with the frame and that maybe the saddleback was added. Once people find out about the original paint they are left with little to say.

One could ponder over this situation for another 14 years and come up with many theories, but as I said earlier, the proof is in the pudding. The best thing that could have ever happened in regards to this situation came about in July of 2014 when my friend J.C. Davidson of Racine, Wisconsin told me to check out a slant guard that was up for auction on eBay. Little did he know when he told me to check it out that it would be the answer I had been searching for years to find.

The slant guard that came out of the woodwork and up for auction was in original red paint with its fair share of surface rust. It was frame serial number 103149 with engine serial number 100114. The frame is two digits above my frame and the engine is one digit below mine. I contacted the seller to confirm the serial numbers. The bike is currently owned by Jesse Buckley in the state of Washington.

What does this information prove? It certainly proves that saddle backs exist well into the 3,000 serial number range. It also proves that low number engines came on high number frames and that the frames and engines do not have to be close in number sequence to be considered a factory match.

Okay, so I know what you are thinking - those two bikes are the only two bikes that have high serial number frames with low serial number engines and that does not prove much. Pete Klein of Iowa owns frame number 103097 with engine number 100183, certainly close to the two mentioned above and an interesting piece to the puzzle. Scott Woody owns an original red slant guard 6 numbers away from mine. His frame serial number is 103141 with engine number 100171.

In July of 2015, a slant guard showed up on eBay in original red paint. It was frame number 103100 with engine number 100054. The interesting thing about this particular original bike was that it is not a saddle back frame. The engine has the early Z50M verbiage oil/clutch cover which has been consistent on the low digit engine serial numbers. Two serial numbers in a row is great evidence but I always said the icing on the cake would be to find engine number 113 or 116.

In September of 2015 Rick Ramsey of Utah purchased frame number 103110 with engine number 100113 to complete the sequence of three serial numbers in a row, something that over the years has been more and more difficult to find.

What does this prove? I believe that it proves that frames were built, piled on racks and later stamped as they were pulled from the rack. Earlier production frames did not necessarily receive the lowest serial number stampings. In my experience, all of the early tall-bar bikes have had the earliest parts on them aside from the oil/clutch cover. The '68 on the sales brochure does not feature the Z50M oil/clutch cover. This is likely because Honda used up the left over covers and some ended up on higher serial number frames as stated earlier.

The question many Mini Trail enthusiasts are looking for the answer to is; how many saddle

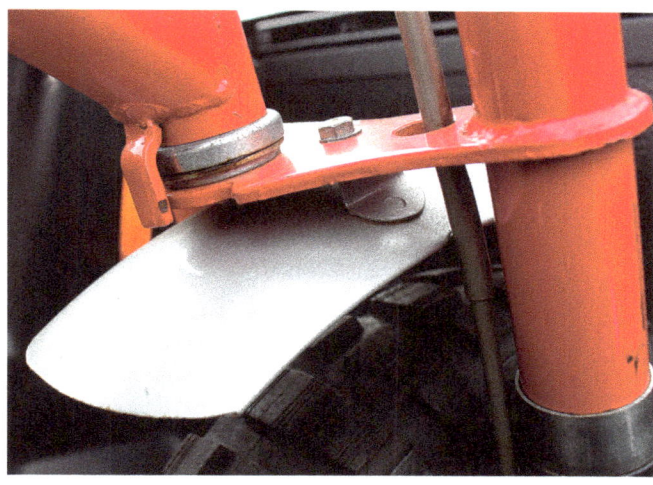

Type I Spot welded mounting bracket front fender.

Type II riveted mounting bracket front fender.

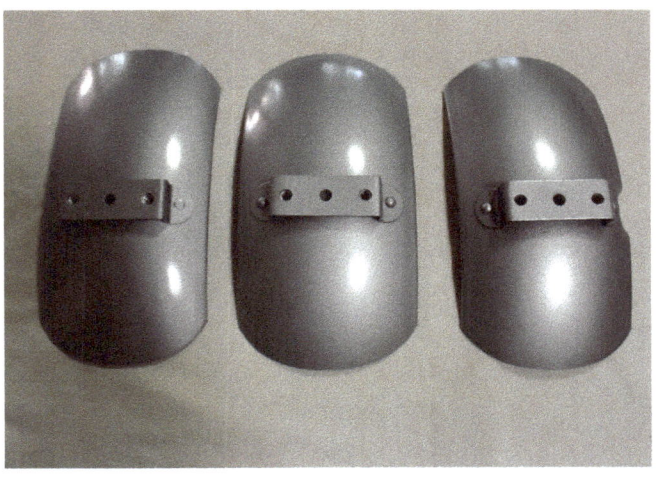

Left to Right, Type 1, type II, type III front fenders.

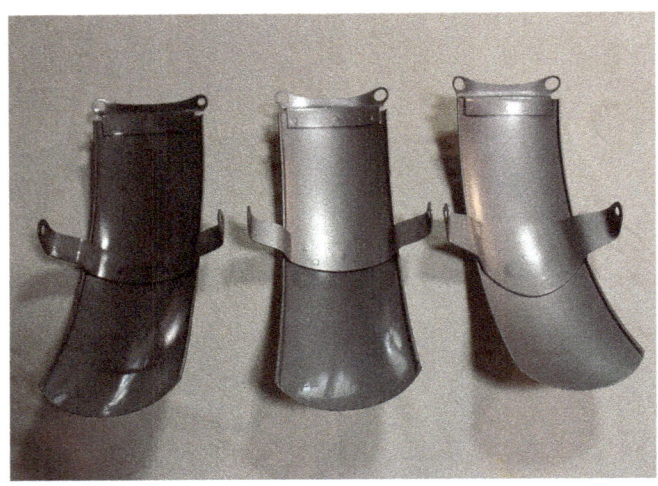

Left to right: Type I rear fender, Type II rear fender & Type III rear fender.

Type I rear fender with small bolt holes that do not require rubber grommets. Used on the following serial number Mini Trails. 100001-103192. This fender requires two 6x12 hex bolts and two 6mm plain washers.

Type II rear fender with large holes to fit black rubber grommets. Requires shoulder bolts. Used on the following serial number Mini Trails. 103193-200087.)

backs were made? The best answer I can give is, nobody knows for sure. However, in my experience, all Mini Trails at serial number 101016 and below has the saddle back. After serial number 101016 it appears that a handful of frames are mixed in and that is what makes this early model so fun and interesting. It doesn't just stop at the frame; there are plenty of other interesting oddities that exist.

A few other interesting features on the '68 frames compared to the other hardtails is that the rear chain adjuster mounting ears have 4 hash markings in the frame for adjusting the chain and the later K1s and K2s have 5.

The '68 frames as well as all K1 frames up to serial number 173239 had flat gas tank mounting tabs on each side of the back bone. The tabs were covered with slotted black rubber mounting pieces that helped hold the gas tank snuggly in place. Today the tabs are often times bent or broken off so it is no wonder why they were switched to a sturdier round tab.

Frame & Engine V.I.N Numbers:

Most motorcycles have a serial number or frame I.D. tag mounted on the steering head tube or a V.I.N number stamped into it. All '68 Z50As came without an I.D. tag. The frame number on a '68 Z50A is stamped on the left side of the rear wheel axle bracket.

The engine serial number is located on the left side of the engine at the bottom just above the shifter. The first 1968 Mini Trail frame is number 100001 and the last is 120087. The first '68 engine serial number is also 100001 and the last serial number is 1200087. However, these engine numbers are certainly not completely accurate because some later serial number engines ended up being used on early production K1s, (more on this topic in the K1 section). The Mini Trail featured in the owner's manual is frame number 100016 with engine number 100085.

How to read a V.I.N tag: The first number on the '68 V.I.N is a 1 and to figure out the production number you count backwards from the last digit. Serial number 105275 is the 5,275th Mini Trail made. Out of all of the frames that were produced up to serial number 105306 with the slant muffler guard protector, within those frames a portion of them had what are referred to by collectors and enthusiasts as the "tall handle bars". The part numbers are: 53100-045-670 right steering handle and 53120-045-670 left steering handle.

The August '68 Honda parts book issue number one references that the Mini Trails with frame serial numbers 100001-101125 required the tall handle bars. What is interesting about this figure is that the parts book is supposed to let the parts departments know exactly which frames required the tall handle bars. If the number was not definitive then the parts department would not have known which bar or bars to order if it were not for the exact serial number ranges in the parts book. Could a serial number above 101126 have a set of tall bars? Based on the serial number range and the fact that the number is definitive and considering the fact that this correction went into the parts book long before the units went on sale I would say no. However, as you may have figured out by now anything is possible. I personally have never seen an all-original Z50A with tall bars above serial number 101126.

Another high point of interest is the tall bars themselves and why they were used, and later dropped from production. They are the only parts in the first edition of the Honda parts book that have a serial number reference as a parts change. Why the bars were changed seems to be a common question of interest with Mini Trail enthusiasts.

The Z50A was built for younger riders and the bars were simply too tall for the target audience. The bars made the unit difficult to ride for the younger crowd and when the bike tipped over the bars bent easily. The change to the shorter style bars seemed to be the trend in the Mini Trail world until the end of production in 1999. The only exception to the rule was in 1979 when Honda went with a taller style bar again. Unlike the '68, the '79 handlebar was used on all units in that model year. After one year of tall bars they too were phased out for the remaining production of the Z50R line.

Frame serial numbers 101126-120087 required what are known today as the "short bars" or standard size bars. All '68 right side handlebars have a hole on the inside of the bar for the throttle cable to exit.

Type I and Type II thin strap center mounting bracket.

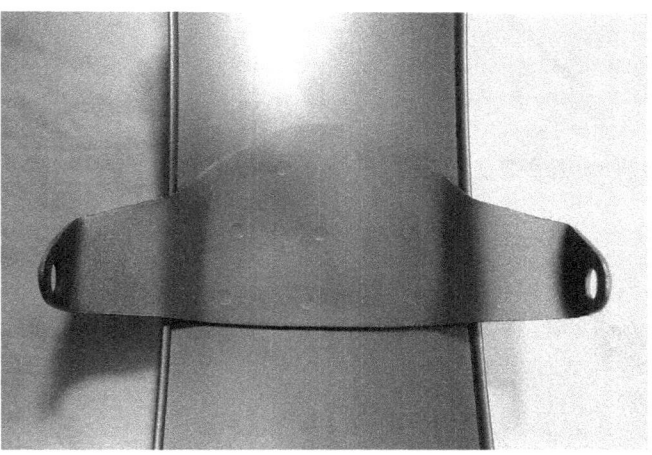

Type III wide center mounting bracket. This bracket is similar to the K1 bracket and this was sold as a Honda service replacement part, not actually used on a factory production Mini Trail

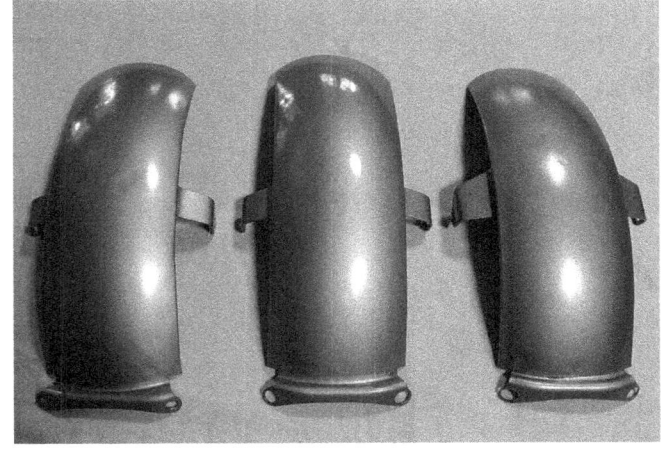

Left to right: Type I rear fender, Type II rear fender & Type III rear fender.

A non-verbiage split bracket muffler found on the 128th Z50A. Jerry Ure Jr. Collection.

Early split bracket muffler, under 4,000 produced.

Straight Guard muffler protector. Frames 105307-120087.

Original handlebars have a low shine flash chrome unlike the modern version of bars currently floating around that were produced by Honda that have triple chrome plating, lever perches that are mounted at an angle, and the bars themselves are tipped back towards the rider.

In all of my years of collecting I have only spotted around 15 or so authentic sets of tall handlebars either on bikes or loose.

Over the last several years, restoration enthusiasts have restored Mini Trails with remade tall bars by taking two sets of handlebars and welding a center section into the middle of one of the sets.

Front Fender:

All Z50As had high no-clog front fenders painted in Cloud Silver. There are three versions of the front fender.

Type I: This fender has the mounting bracket spot welded on and no cable notch. Most of these fenders had the spot welds that came loose and if you find them today many are bolted together or pop riveted back on. The spot welded front fender is among the rarest of all Mini Trail parts. This fender has been found on frame numbers 100128 100609, 100645, 100659, 100720, 100797, 100799, 100896, 1003147 and 104332.

Type II: This is a pop-riveted style fender with no cable notch in it on the kicker side of the fender. This is the most common type of fender found on straight guards. This fender has been found on slant guard frame number 105203 as well as every straight guard I have ever seen. When exactly did this fender come into production remains a mystery. However, based on my research it began somewhere in the mid 4,000 serial number range.

Type III: This is a later model service replacement part. This fender was later made by Honda and it has a side notch in the fender for the front brake cable and it looks like the mid-production K1 style fender. The color used on this later style fender is the later version of Honda Cloud Silver; it has a darker tone and a metal flake.

The fender will bolt on perfectly and serve its purpose but this part is not correct for a restoration or an original Mini Trail. The reason being is that this fender was not found on production Mini

Trails. Like many current issue Honda parts today, this fender is a cross over between the original Z50A style fender and the later K1 style fender.

Rear Fender:

The rear fender is a very interesting part to say the least. All Z50As came equipped with a high no-clog rear fender painted in cloud silver. Like the front, there are three versions of the rear fender.

Type I: This fender has spot welds holding the narrow center bracket in place and is a direct mounting fender with small oval holes for the mounting bolts. This style fender does not require the rubber mounting grommets and uses standard #8 non-shoulder bolts and 6mm washers.

According to the January 25th, 1969 Honda parts manual issue Number 2, only the first 3,192 Z50A's required this type of fender. Z50A frame numbers 100867, 100797, 100896, 101016, and 103147 came with the solid mounted type I rear fender, which fits perfectly within the Honda production figures.

Type II: According to the January 25th 1969 Honda parts manual issue number 2, this fender was supposed to go on all Mini Trails from serial number 103193 to 120087. This fender has a narrow center bracket but it is slightly wider than the type I fender center bracket and uses the rubber grommets and shoulder bolts to mount the fender to the bottom of the frame.

Just like the tall handle bars, this part has a definitive serial number range. Based on the numbers, 3,192 slant guards came with the type I rear fender, while 2,114 slant guards and 14,781 straight guards came with the type II rear fender. My Norm Reeves yellow slant guard (# 104332) has a grommet rear fender with shoulder bolts, proof that the early fender came and went early in the production run.

Type III: This fender is the service replacement fender in cloud silver. This style fender never came on a production Mini Trail. It requires lower rubber mounting grommets, uses the same mounting hardware as the type II fender and the entire center bracket is wide and looks similar to the K1 style center bracket.

Muffler

Typically, most collectors have been under the

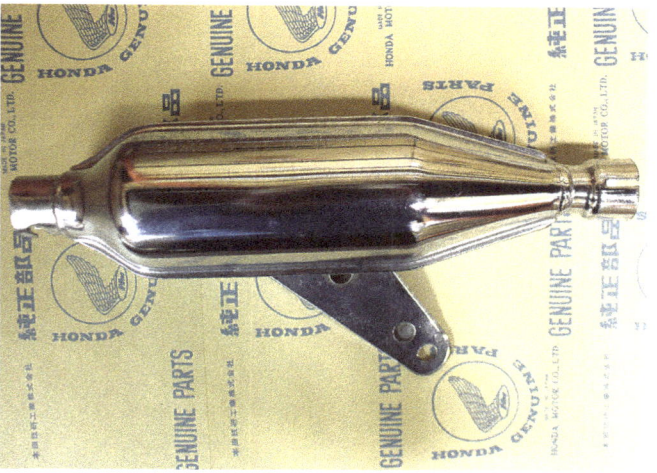

A fused bracket muffler. Found on late Slant Guards and all straight guards.

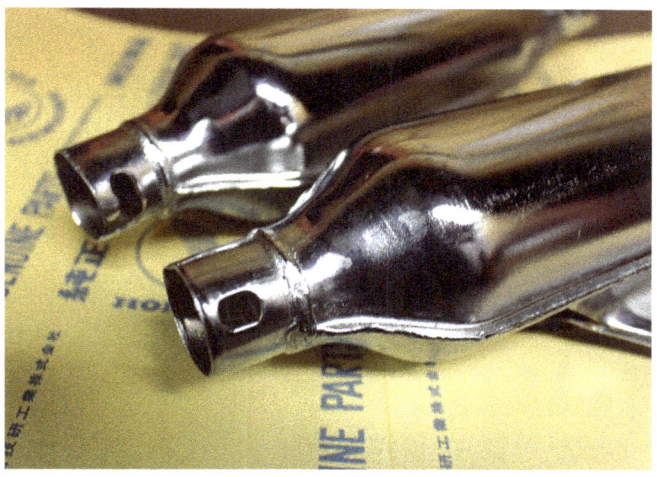

Top muffler: Notch in muffler end for Z50A diffuser. Bottom muffler: No notch cut out. This is found on the 128th muffler and most K1's and all K2's.

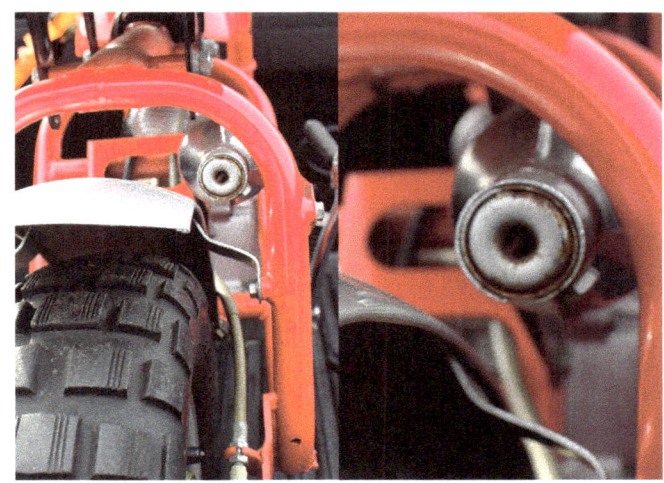

Early pencil-hole muffler diffuser with a thin metal bar inside the diffuser. Most commonly found on Slant Guards.

Left to right: Type II diffuser, most commonly found on Slant Guards. Type III diffuser, most commonly found on straight guards.

Left to right: Type III diffuser with large outlet hole. Type III diffuser mounted on a 14,000 serial number range Z50A.

Pat. Pend muffler verbiage. This is found on all Z50A's except on the 128th Mini Trail. Also found on early K1's.

assumption that there are two variations of the '68 mufflers. A third variation has been found on frame number 100128 fitted with engine number 100032. This style muffler has the split mounting bracket, however the U.S. patent pending text that is common verbiage on '68 mufflers is NOT printed on the muffler. The muffler oddly enough does not have a notch cut out in it like the mid run K1s and all K2s for the diffuser to turn in and lock. The muffler has not been re-chromed and currently is in beautiful original condition. Currently Jerry Ure Jr. owns this muffler and he believes that maybe the muffler was intended to be used on a European model since the text was left off. He explains that, "If you order a muffler from Honda today it does not come with any text on it". It could also have been an error and it slipped through production without any text on it. It also could have been a sample or a pre-production part that found its way into production. Whatever the case may be it certainly is a rare piece and a great conversation starter.

The second style muffler is a split mounting bracket type and it includes Patent Pending verbiage. The split muffler bracket has been found on many of the earliest style Mini Trails and has been found on many slant guard models, but certainly not all. Frame numbers 100609, 100645, 100797, 100799, 102992, 100867, 100896, 100992, 103147, and 103149 originally came with this style split bracket muffler.

When did the split bracket muffler go away? Norm Reeves Honda of California sold Jack Ortiz a yellow and white slant guard with frame number 104332 on November 29th 1968 and it does not have the split bracket muffler. Ken Peare of New Jersey owns slant guard frame number 104176 and it does not have the split bracket muffler. Frame number 105302, one of the last slant guards ever made does not have a split bracket muffler either. Frame number 1003147 and frame number 103149 both have split bracket mufflers. Frame number 103852 does not have a split bracket muffler. Based on the serial number examples I have concluded that the split bracket muffler went away somewhere between frame numbers 103150 and 103851.

The third style muffler is a spot welded fused together bracket similar to the K1 and K2 bracket and it is faced with patent pending verbiage. Slant guard frame numbers 104176 and 104332 as well as straight guard frame numbers 116960 and 117234 have this style muffler. This is the most common muffler found on the '68. This muffler looks like a K1 muffler less the patent number and the long diffuser.

Diffusers:

If the muffler situation isn't confusing enough, it gets more confusing when you factor in the different diffusers found on the '68 Z50As. Other than the muffler on Jerry's Mini Trail, all Z50A mufflers came with a notch for a plug style diffuser. The diffuser pushed in, twisted until locked in place and it is secured with a 5mm bolt and flat, zinc-plated washer.

No actual tail pipe stuck out like on the K1 and K2 models, this type of diffuser mounted flush with the end of the muffler. Some Mini Trail collectors refer to the diffuser as a donut plug or donut stinger.

There are at least three variations of the diffuser found on the '68.

Type I: This version is found on frame number 100128. This is a wide open diffuser with a thin center bar. This diffuser came in the non-verbiage muffler.

Type II: This is the baffle bar style similar to what is found on the trail 70's and the outlet hole is about the size of a pencil. This very restrictive style diffuser is what gives the '68 a popping sound when it is idling. This style is found on frame numbers 100217, 100609, 100645, 100896, 102992, 103147, 104176, and 104332. Based on the wide range of serial numbers it seems to be the most common type found on slant guards. These have been reproduced and are easy to spot because the inner ring in the tube has been machined out of a solid piece of metal rather than welded into the tube and the center bar is not present when looking through the outlet hole.

Type III: This version is known by collectors as the large donut hole diffuser. This stinger is the most commonly found version on straight guards. This style diffuser has been reproduced so when

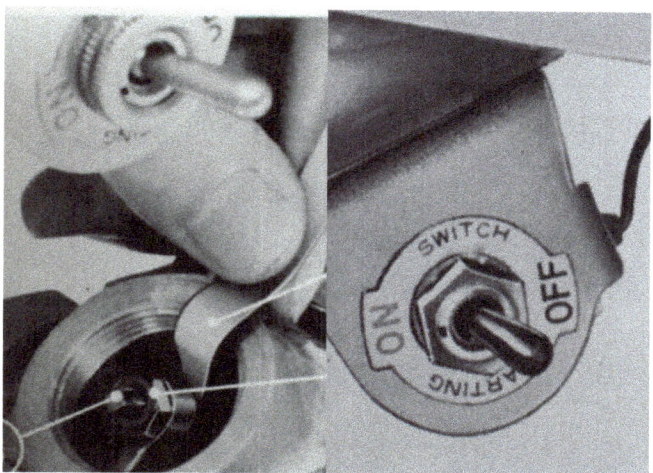

Pictures of toggle switches from the original owner's manual. Evidence that two versions of the toggle switch existed before sales took place.

Type I toggle switch with hex nut and engraved switch plate.

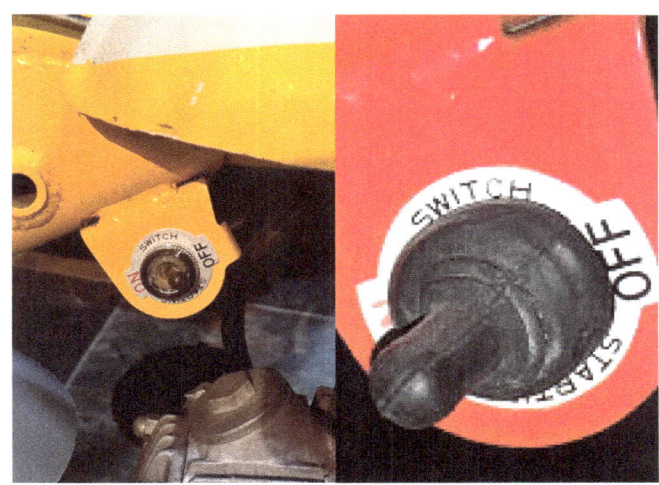

Left to right: Type II knurled nut and silk screened switch plate. Type III silk screened switch plate with rubber cover.

Factory Bright Yellow or Scarlet Red touch-up paint came with each Mini Trail.

Late Z50A 1968 tank showing the paddle mark on the bottom from the dipping process.

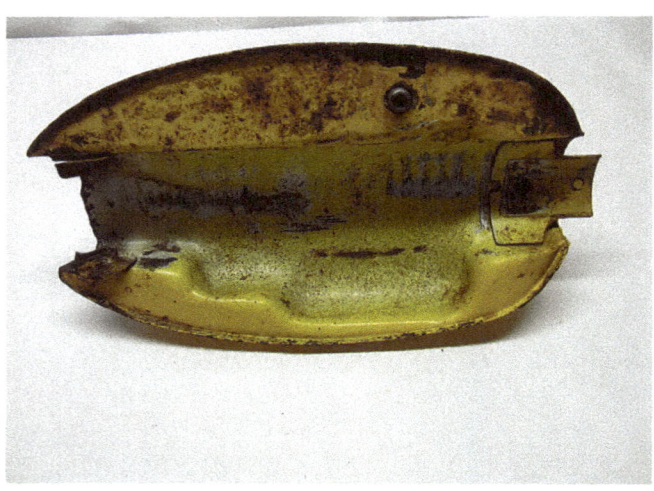

Early Z50A tank showing that they were sprayed and not dipped.

attempting to do a 100-point restoration beware of reproduction diffusers. The originals are a two-piece unit fused together in the center and the reproductions are a one piece tapered tube. These are around in small quantities since only a few private individuals have reproduced them.

Toggle Switch:

All '68 Z50A's came with a one-wire on/off toggle kill switch. There were two versions of the toggle switch. However, the way they were outfitted on the bikes gives them multiple combinations in physical appearance.

Type I: It has a chrome plate with engraved wording on it. This toggle switch is present on frame numbers 100609, 100645, 100797, 100896, 103147, and 104332. This came with a thin threaded nut and washer to hold the on/off plate and the toggle to the frame. Many Mini Trail enthusiasts refer to this as the early style toggle switch.

Where it gets interesting is when you look at frame number 100217 with engine number 100334. This Mini Trail came with the type II toggle switch plate. It is a silk-screened lettering type of toggle plate. This particular early Mini Trail still has the thin threaded nut to hold the plate on. Frame number 105203 has the thin threaded nut and an engraved switch plate.

In all of my research, most slant guards came with the simple brass nut and washer to hold on the toggle switch plate. However, when looking through my September 1968 owner's manual I noticed that on page 23 it shows the small brass nut and on page 35 it shows the knurled nut. The owner's manual pictures provide proof that both versions existed right away in production. It is important to keep in mind that many early pre-production pictures from sales brochures, magazine ads, or owner's manuals are not always typical of production items.

Type 2: The second version of the type II toggle plate came with a knurled nut to hold the on/off plate and the toggle to the frame. The knurled nut silk-screen version is the most common toggle switch. It is the most commonly used version of the toggle switch and is the version you will most likely find if you were to find an NOS one for sale.

The knurled nut chrome plate version of the toggle switch exists in NOS form, however, I have yet to see this combination on an actual Mini Trail but it does not mean that it does not exist.

Type 3: The third version of the toggle was identical to the Type II switch. However, because people were supposedly being shocked when trying to turn off the Mini Trail, Honda added a little rubber cover to go over the knurled nut. Another theory is that it helped keep dirt out of the switch as well. This rubber cover type was found on frame number 112058.

Gas Tank:

The gas tanks were made out of metal and came in two colors: Scarlet Red on the bottom and Ivory White on the top. The other color combination was Bright Yellow on the bottom and Ivory White on the top.

There are three styles of the gas tank for the production bikes and one type of service replacement tank in the two production colors. Almost all '68s had welded filler neck tanks. Wait, what? The people in the know believe that all '68 fuel tanks had welded neck gas tanks and that all K1s and K2s did not. Let's take a look.

Type 1: The first style tank is a welded filler neck type tank with sprayed on paint. The area around the filler neck where the gas cap screws on has a bead of weld around it. The welded style filler necks did not have every inch of them covered in the ivory white paint; but rather they looked like they were missing paint in the pockets in the welds. Sometimes the weld was very thin and not as noticeable as others. Or sometimes there is no weld at all and this is evident on frame/tank number 100128 owned by Jerry Ure. Jr.

Frame numbers 100609 and 100896 both have vibrant original paint on them and it is very evident that these tanks were not dipped, but rather sprayed from the factory. Evidence is the fuzzy paint lines, the bleeding on the front shifter side corner of the tank by the steering tube, the absence of the paddle mark on the bottom of the tank, and the most convincing evidence is the original masking tape still stuck to the bottom of the tank on frame number 100896.

The early style tanks were painted Ivory White

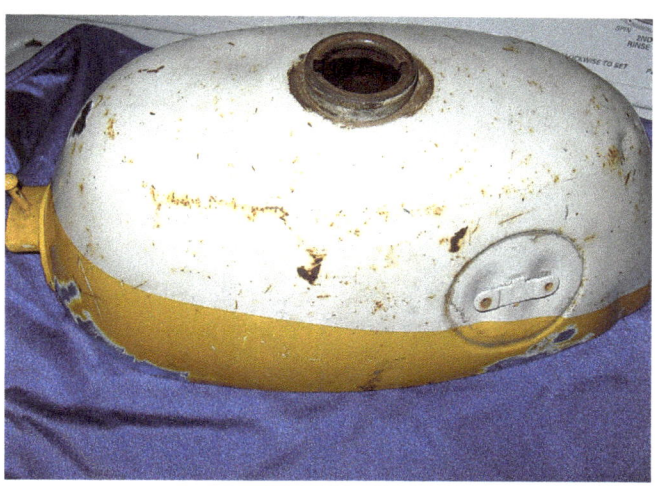

Late Z50A tank without a welded filler neck.

A spray painted early production tank from frame number 128. Later tanks were dipped. Jerry Ure Jr. Collection.

The fuel neck from the above gas tank showing that there is no weld around the filler neck.

1968 Z50A and K1 round tank emblems. Chrome screws with punch dot marks. Modern screws from Honda come with cross marks instead of dot punch marks.

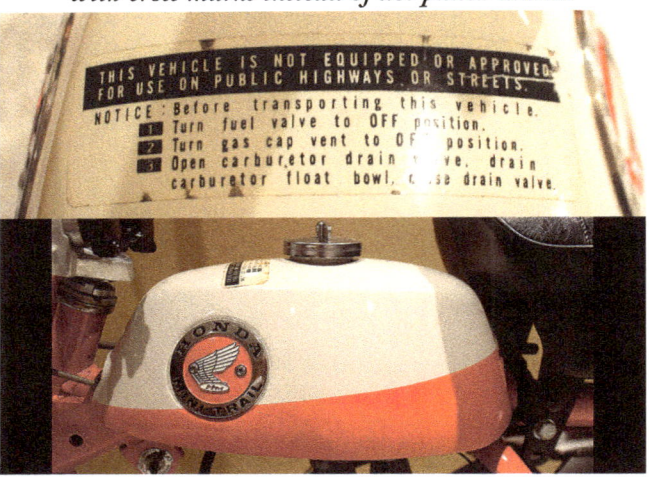

1968 Z50A exclusive transporting tank decal.

Type I seat.

at first, masked, and then sprayed. Evidence of this procedure is best witnessed on the tank from frame number 100896. The bottom of the tank shows the red over spray on the white and as previously mentioned, the factory masking tape is still present on the tank.

The interesting thing about the bottom of the tank on Mini Trail 609 is that it has a serial number stamped into it. The number reads, 80712. This is the only tank I have ever seen with a number stamped into the bottom of the tank. I believe the number to mean that the tank was built on July 12th of 1968 or 07/12/68.

Type 2: The second style tank is also a welded filler neck tank. The later style welded neck tanks appear to have a cleaner weld around the filler necks. Most notably these tanks underwent a dipping process to apply the paint. Later style welded neck tanks had the paddle mark design paint scheme on the bottom of the tank like all K1/K2 bikes. The tanks were dipped at the factory and that is why they have the paddle mark design on the bottom. They called it a paddle mark because of the fixture that held it during the paint application process. Other evidence that they were dipped is the beaded paint along the bottom edge of the tank.

Many die hard restoration buffs spend time measuring the side stripe line on the side of the tank when restoring their bikes because they want to get it just right. The reality is that since the tanks were dipped, it all depended on how much paint was left in the vat in determining how high the back tank stripe line was going to be and how low the front tank stripe line would end up. They were mass produced mini bikes for kids so rest assured that there is no exact science or precision as to how they turned out.

Type 3: The third style tank that was used on factory production models was the non-welded neck tank. This version of the tank has the filler neck welded from the bottom side like the welded neck tanks but does not have the bead of weld around the filler neck. This version of the tank was dipped rather than sprayed.

The final version of the tank is the service replacement tank. These tanks were painted all ivory white on the bottom and thus no paddle mark paint design. They had a stamped filler neck with one tiny side weld, certainly different than the factory K1 and K2 stamped filler necks but none the less they were still stamped filler necks.

Tank Warning Decal and Badges

Like most motorcycles, they feature safety warning or instructional decals. The '68 tank came with a decal that outlined the steps for the operator when transporting the unit. The decal was clear in nature with black text. The main difference in the '68 decal from the K1 decal is that the '68 does not have step 4 on it, which talks about the battery removal process for transportation purposes.

Regarding badges, the '68 came with a round badge on each side of the tank that said "Honda" on top and "Mini Trail" on the bottom with the signature wing in the center. The badges were Chrome, red, and white, with Honda in black letters. The badges were secured to the tank with two chrome Phillips headed 3mm screws. Each screw has a punch mark on the head for ISO identification.

Seat:

My favorite part of any motorcycle is the seat, just ask collector Gregg Davidian about me and my love for high quality original seats. The condition of the seat usually tells a story in relation to the condition of the motorcycle.

For me it is the one part that, when trying to do a proper restoration, usually can't be duplicated because perfect original seats are far and few between and usually are still on quality motorcycles.

All '68s came with a two-hole position adjustable style seat post frame assembly with two-wire spark plug wrench holders underneath. The seat came in black vinyl in two design styles with two different types of foam pads and a non-reinforced seat pan.

Type I: This is the holy grail of all Mini Trail parts! This seat has 6 top seams, low kick style foam, a seam up the front of the cover, no seam in the rear, and a Honda logo in silver on the back. This seat is the one that is featured on the sales brochure, in the owner's manual, and various other magazine publications that featured the Z50A. The

Type II seat.

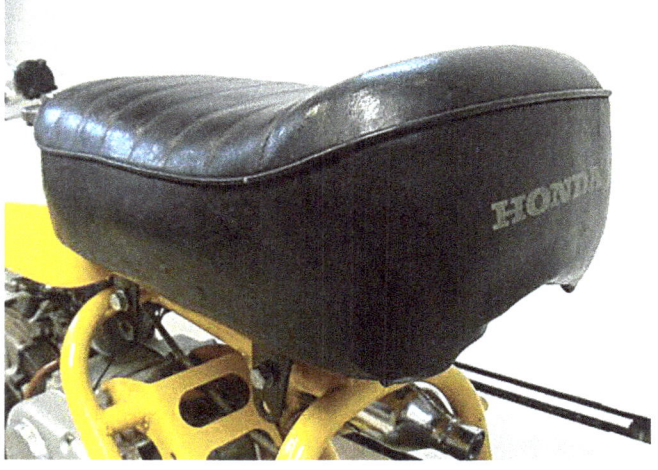

Type III seat.

Seat brackets mounted directly to the seat pan. Z50A to early K1's used this seat pan.

31

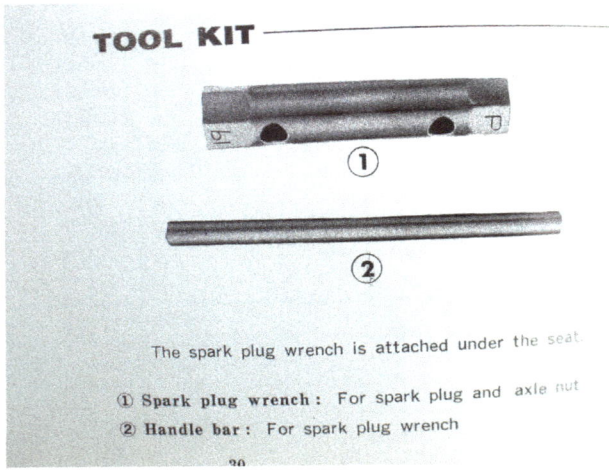

Owner's manual photo showing the double-sided spark plug wrench.

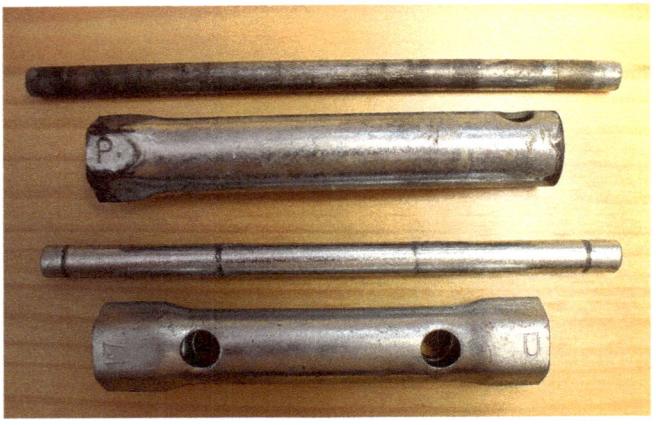

Top wrench: Single sided wrench found under the seats of the majority of hard tails. Bottom wrench: Double sided wrench found under the seat of frame number 100609. The only one known to exist. Jeremy Polson Collection.

The 1st 6,900, Z50As used a 34 tooth rear sprocket. Frames 6,901-20,087 used a 35 tooth rear sprocket.

only Mini Trail that I have ever seen with this style seat is frame # 100609. How many still exist today remains a mystery. I have a suspicion that since I have no pictures or know of anyone with any Mini Trails in the 100225-100600 range that it is likely that there was a run of this style seat mixed in this serial number range.

The December of 1968 Cycle World Magazine shows a slant guard with a 6-seam seat. My guess is that a small batch of the seats were made and it remains a mystery as to how many were actually made. As of now I am the only one in the world known to have one! (Not to be confused with the rear split seam K1 or K2 seats that are 6-seam) If anybody has one of these seats, please come forward!

Type II: This seat has 7 top seams, low kick style foam, a seam up the front of the cover, no seam in the rear, and a Honda logo in silver on the back. This seat is found on frame numbers 100070, 100217, 100645, 100659, 100720, 100797, 100799, 100992, 102992, 103147, 104176, 104332, and 105302. Other than the 6-seam seat, this is the only other seat found on Slant guards.

Type III: This seat has 7 seams, high kick style foam with the seam up the front of the seat with a Honda logo in silver on the back without a rear seam. This seat was most likely designed to keep kids from falling off the back. This high kick foam design carried on throughout the production of the K1 and K2. This seat is found on frame number 116960, 116729, and 117234.

Tool Kit:

The '68 seat came with two-wire tool kit clips fastened to the bottom of the seat with 10mm nuts. The tool kit is simple, just a tube and a bar. All '68s at frame number 108295 and below came with the 89216-045-670 sparking plug wrench and it was a double sided wrench that on one side said "P" for tightening or loosening the spark plug and the other side said "19" for tightening or loosening the front and rear axle nuts.

All '68 Mini Trails from frame number 108296 and beyond came with the single sided wrench tube that said "P" on the end. This was the same wrench that was used on the K1s and K2s as well. Or so the parts book says on the wrenches. The only 1968 that I have ever seen with the double-sided wrench is frame number 100609. There are modern versions of the wrench with a punched hole in the center of the wrench. All other '68s I have come across have had the single sided wrench.

Seat Pan:

The '68 Z50A seat pan features two brackets mounted directly to the thin metal seat pan with very minimal tack welds. A poor design that was corrected later in the Z50A K1 production. The revised version of the seat pan featured a wide metal plate welded directly to the bottom of the seat pan. The seat mounting brackets were then welded to the support plate for strength. It is very common to see a '68 seat with a cracked or busted seat pan because many people either rode double or lifted the seat from the back, thus putting stress on the thin seat brackets and cracking the pan.

Rear Sprocket:

Two versions of rear sprockets were found on production '68s. According to the Honda parts manual and microfiche as of January 1969, a 34-tooth sprocket was intended for frame number ranges 100001-106900. The second version was a 35 tooth rear sprocket and it was intended for frame ranges 106901-120087. Both versions had a zinc plated "kidney bean" hole style sprocket with a three-hole bolt pattern.

There were optional higher tooth sprockets you could order to change up the gear ratio. A 38 tooth sprocket was usually the most common upgrade, however a 42 and a 46 tooth sprocket could also be ordered.

Rear Sprocket Lock Washers:

Two versions of the rear sprocket lock washer were used on the '68.

Type 1: The first version, found on all slant guards and some straight guards were the three separate lock washers. This set up was used to hold each sprocket bolt in place. The tabs that hold each bolt in place are squared on each corner.

As of the January 29th 1969 a Honda service bulletin was issued that changed the previous parts to a one-piece setup. The August of '68 parts book does not show the three piece set up, but rather it shows three separate tooth washers, these were

Left to right: 420 thickness sprocket versus a 415 thickness. Optional sprockets that could be dealer installed came in 38, 42, or 46 teeth.

Early Z50A's used three individual sprocket lock washers. Later they were switched to a one-piece unit.

415 chains were used on all 1968 Z50A's.

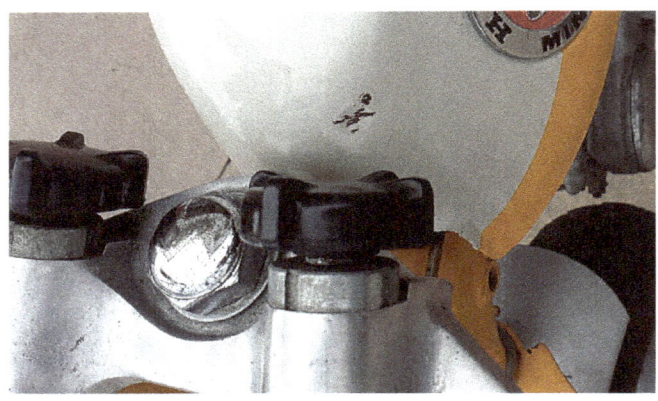

Early triple clamp with rough metal around the steering stem nut.

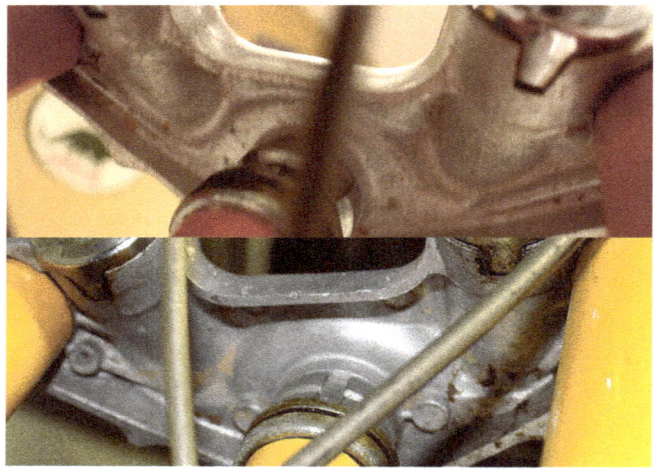

Top clamp: Type I clamp without brace supports or mold markings. Bottom clamp: Type II with mold markings and without bracing.

Left to right: Nitto brand tires used on the 1st Z50A's produced and the majority of them after. Some Bridgestone tires have been spotted on late 1968 Z50A's.

never used on the production Mini Trails. The January of 1969 parts book shows the one-piece tongued washer.

Type 2: The second version found only on straight guards as well as the K1s and K2s is the one-piece tongued washer. The tabs on the original one-piece tongue washer are also squared-off on the corners.

A modern version of the one piece tongued washer is still available, however it has rounded corners.

Front Sprocket:

Each rear sprocket had a special front sprocket to go with it. According to the Honda Parts manual and microfiche of '69 the 13-tooth drive sprocket was intended for frame ranges 100001-106900. The 12-tooth was intended for frame ranges 106901-120087.

The 13-tooth drive sprocket required the 23802-041-000 drive sprocket fixing plate, again this was up to frame number 106900. The later 12-tooth drive sprocket required the 23802-065-305 drive sprocket fixing plate on all engines after serial number 106901.

Chain:

All Z50As came equipped with a 74 link 415 style chain. The 415 chain is a smaller style chain than the later model hardtails, and is often said to resemble a bicycle chain. If a larger rear sprocket was added, two more links per sprocket size were required.

Fork Top Clamp:

Early Mini Trails did not have webbing supports to strengthen the bottom of the clamp. Clamps often times cracked in the center. This was later corrected with center webbing, which was added for more support.

Two versions of the non-webbed triple clamp exist.

Type I: Slant guard frame #104176 has the non-webbed clamp as do all of the other slant guards that I have seen below this serial number. The non-reinforced clamps have a marking on the bottom that says "E 1 or E 2". This design was a carry-over from the 1967 Z50M. Frame numbers 100609 and 100896 have the E2 marking on the bottom of the clamp.

Pete Klein of Iowa owns five '68s and he has two straight guards in the 8,000 and 9,000 serial number range and they both have E1 and E2 clamps with the 9,000 serial number bike having the E1 clamp.

Another unique feature on these clamps is the area where the large washer and center mounting nut attaches. It is not smooth or polished in this area like the later style '68 clamps and all of the K1 and K2 clamps, but rather rough and porous. How many Mini Trails used this style clamp is uncertain. However, based on my research it certainly outlasted the split bracket muffler, the tall bars, and the type I fenders.

Type II: This triple clamp is also a non-webbed clamp and this time they were polished in the center top section where the steering stem nut goes. The most noticeable feature on the type II clamp is that it has circle mold marks on the bottom. This style clamp is most commonly found on straight guard '68s.

Handle Holder Nuts and Knobs

The handle holder nuts that were used on the '68 were smooth on the backside. Later in the hardtail line of production there were hollow pockets in the face.

The black handle holder twist knobs underwent a change just after the slant guard. All frames at 105766 and below used the 53741-045-020 twist knob and all frames at 105767 and beyond used the 53741-045-304 twist knob.

Cables

Gray brake cables without brake light switches were used on all '68 models. The throttle cable is gray as well. The cables are marked with the black "TSK" markings and say made in Japan in black.

The original rear cables had a red identification number stamped in them down by the rubber boot on the casing. The front brake cables did not have the red markings nor did the throttle cables. Both front and rear original cables that came on the Mini Trails can be distinguished from NOS cables by the diamond logo on the top of the rubber boot.

The replacement cables from Honda have a red part number stamped into them if they are gray and if they are the later style replacement cables in black they have a white part number. Red bands

Ivory white grips, Ivory white plastic levers, and tall handle bars. Tall bars used on the 1st 1,125 Mini Trails.

Cloud Silver wheels, big "8" wheel bolts on first 8,925 units, and double nutted valve stems.

Dill Brand air caps used on original Nitto inner tubes. Dill caps are present on both of my original tall bar Mini Trails.

35

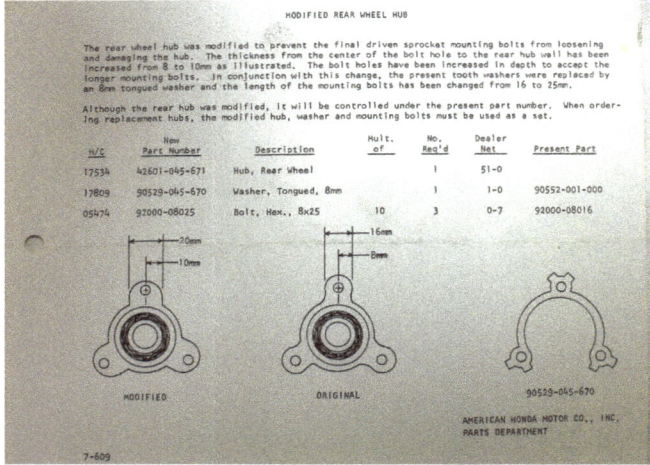

January of 1969 Honda service bulletin explaining the new stronger rear hub, longer bolts, and one-piece sprocket lock washer.

Left to right: NGK spark plug cap used on all 1968 Z50A's. Thin blade gas cap, Z50M, Z50A, and K1.

Long tail flywheel cover used on all Z50M's, Z50A's, and early K1s.

on the bottom of front brake cables are common on the replacement new old stock cables and the red band was not found on factory original cables mounted on early Mini Trails.

Honda ran a line of black replacement cables and they were readily available in the 1990s. There are reproduction gray cables that say Honda Z50 K0 in white on them as well.

Center nut:

The steering stem center nut used on the '68 is a lower profile nut in thickness than the current issue center nut that is available from Honda. If you are trying to do a 100-point restoration or want to keep your bike original, it is important to know the difference in the two parts.

Tires:

Honda used a 3.50-8 inch rugged Nitto tire on most of the '68 Z50As. I have seen two '68s with Bridgestone tires and they were both in original paint. Frame number 117551, as pictured, has them.

Wheels:

All '68s used two-piece round hole cloud silver wheels with four circular holes in them. The owner's manual shows a wheel with large kidney bean holes like the Z50R's from the '80s had. Like most early literature it was used for promotional purposes and often times it varied from the production models.

Inner Tubes

Two brass nuts secured the brass valve stem to the rim dish. The valve stems were at a 90-degree angle. The inner tubes, just like the tires, were Nitto brand tubes or Bridgestone.

Brake Levers

Ivory White plastic hand brake levers were used on all models. The colors seem to vary when NOS levers come up for sale. Original pictures show very stark white-looking levers. I have examined an original sun faded set of levers and the underside portion of them in the area that goes into the lever perch is a bright white color. Reproduction white levers exist and the mold markings are what set them apart from the originals.

Hand Grips

Ivory White rubber hand grips were used on all models. Just like the levers, original pictures show very stark white grips. The problem with finding an NOS set is finding a clean set without any factory imperfections. It is not uncommon to find grips with red dye marks in them or brown stain marks. It is also difficult to find grips that match being that they usually were sold in bags of 5 or 10 per side.

It is very common to see an original set of grips in a yellowish state from years of sun exposure. Modern NOS versions of the grips have a small number "2" on the bottom side of the grip where they are seamed together. The number "2" most likely means second run.

Reproduction white grips exist in many forms. There are black grips vinyl-dyed white. There are bright white grips that are thicker than the originals as well as very rounded on the ends. There are flimsy grips in a yellowish off white color as well.

Front Fork:

All '68 Z50As came with a front fork that had one hole in the center plate so the front brake cable could go directly down to the brake hub and not get tangled into the tire. Being that the bike was intended for off road use only; the front fork did not come with fork reflectors or headlight mounts.

Another difference the K0 fork has when compared to most K1s and all K2s is that it does not have fork leg locks on the top of the fork. This version of the Mini Trail fork requires metal inserts to lock the fork legs in place.

According to the Honda parts book, all Mini Trails at frame number 174447 and below required the fork top seat inserts. With that being said, over 50,000 K1s used the metal inserts as well.

Brake Hubs and Brake Plates:

The front brake hubs on the Z50A came with only 4 support braces on the inside of them whereas the later style hubs featured 8 support braces for added strength. Mounted on the bike nobody would ever be able to tell the difference. But it is a piece of mind knowing you have the correct one that makes collectors go crazy. The first production run of Z50As came with a smaller style rear hub.

As of January 29th 1969 Honda issued a service bulletin stating that the rear wheel hub was modified to prevent the final driven sprocket bolts from loosening and damaging the hub. The

Marble coil used on the Z50M, Z50A, and Z50A K1.

Large drain screw carburetor, a carry-over concept from the Z50M. Also used on early K1's.

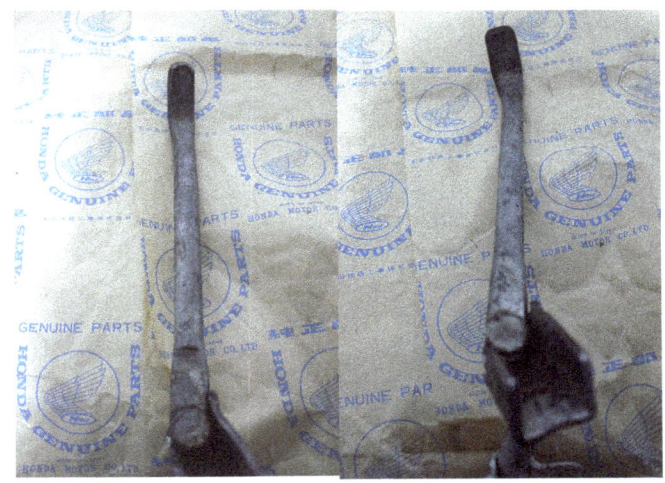

2 versions of the '68 kickstand. Possibly from two different vendors or differences during the production run.

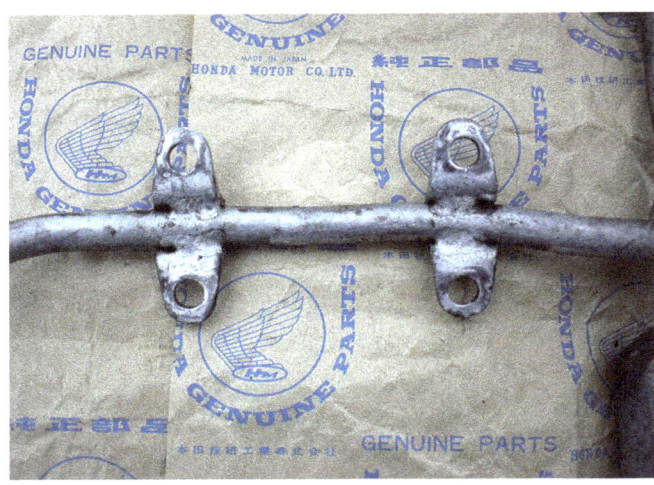

Type I thin diameter step bar.

Type II thick diameter step bar.

Left to right: Early foot peg pillions lacking the double reinforced inner sleeves. 49cc stamped head found on engine number 100992 off of frame number 100609. Some heads did not have 49cc but rather letter and number markings.

thickness from the center of the bolt hole to the outer wall was increased from 8mm to 10mm. The bolt holes have increased in depth as well to accept longer bolts. The bolt holes went from 16mm to 25mm. Honda also replaced the three separate tooth washers with one 8mm tongued washer as mentioned in the sprocket section.

The later model bikes all the way through the K2 model had the larger style rear hub but even the later style hub underwent some changes in physical appearance that will be explained in the K1 section. All of the brake plates were the same from '68-'71. They had a brake arm mounted on a cam on each to pull the front and rear cables. The rear arm was marked with an "R".

Flywheel Magneto Cover:

All '68s had the longer style flywheel magneto cover. Some refer to it as the "long tail cover" or "shark tail cover". The cover is a Cloud Silver painted part with the center section polished with a light clear coat on it like the clear coat on the hubs and brake plates. The Honda wording in the center is not painted black nor is the "made in Japan" text.

Gas Cap and Petcock Valve:

All '68 Z50As came with a chrome gas cap, with a thin butterfly on-off shut-off valve. The caps were engraved with the words ON and OFF. This is a vented style gas cap for transportation purposes.

All '68 Z50As came with the small butterfly petcock fuel valve. This was an On-Off type of valve with no fuel reserve. The filter for straining the gas was a gold colored soft metal filter that was brazed onto the petcock.

Ignition coil/Cap/plug:

All '68 Z50A's came with a marble style ignition coil. All of the original '68s I have come across have had a C-6H NGK spark plug and an NGK cap.

Date-coded parts are not common on Mini Trails like they are on muscle car parts or even the Schwinn Krate bikes, but the interesting fact about the ignition coil is that the spark plug wire on the ignition coil of frame number 100896 in my personal collection has "1968" stamped on it in white. The faces of the coils on frame numbers 100609 as well as 100896 both have the following markings: "M61-09" and "807" stamped in them. Besides the early K1s, most have a 9 as the first digit in the 2nd bubble indicating 1969 production. The number 807 on the coil is actually a production code. The first digit which is an 8 stands for the model year 1968. The next two numbers are the month of production, which in this case is July, the 7th month of the year.

Stator:

All '68 Z50As came with a one-wire stator with a female two prong connector in a clear/yellowish rubber boot. The coil and toggle switch plug into the stator. The stator on a '68 does not have a lighting coil, which started with the K1.

Foot peg Step Bar/Pegs/Kickstand:

There are two versions of the step bar and at least three versions of the kickstand.

Type 1: The first type of step bar is the thin diameter bar with the narrow kickstand. The mounting tabs on this style bar were straight metal pieces as opposed to the later style pegs, which were flared out and resemble butterfly wings. These early style step bars were notorious for bending and tweaking. The fold-up pegs were single strength metal on this version and the rubber pieces had an "HM" logo stamped in them.

Type 2: The second set of foot pegs may either be an attempt at a beefier kickstand or it was a variation from a second vendor producing them at the same time as the other thin bar pegs. This version has the thin center bar but with a wider base kickstand. I own both versions of the early step bars with both kick stands and they are on bikes in the first 3,000 or so made. Just like the other early style step bars, the fold-up pegs were also single strength metal and they too featured the "HM" rubber pieces.

Type 3: The third version of the step bar is the type found on later '68s as well as the K1s and K2s. This version has the thicker center bar and the wider kick stand. The foot peg rubber has an "HM" logo on them. The current version of foot pegs still available from Honda does not have the "HM" logo on the foot peg rubber.

The fold-up foot pegs were not double reinforced with an inner sleeve like the later versions of the pillion pegs found on K1s and K2s. In the January of 1969 Cycle Guide Magazine

Big "8" bolts used on all 1968 Z50A's.

A 1968 Z50A straight guard with original shipping tag and only 5 hours use. Northeast Vintage Cycle Collection.

Z50M verbiage oil clutch cover found on some early serial number engines. The sales brochure Tall Bar does not have this cover.

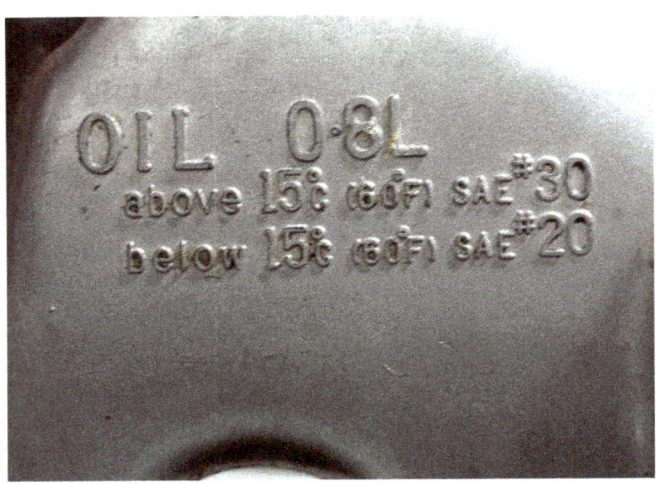

The most common verbiage oil clutch cover found on hard tails.

Round headed zinc plated axles. Z50A frames have 4 hash mark chain adjustment lines. Later switched to 5 during K1 production.

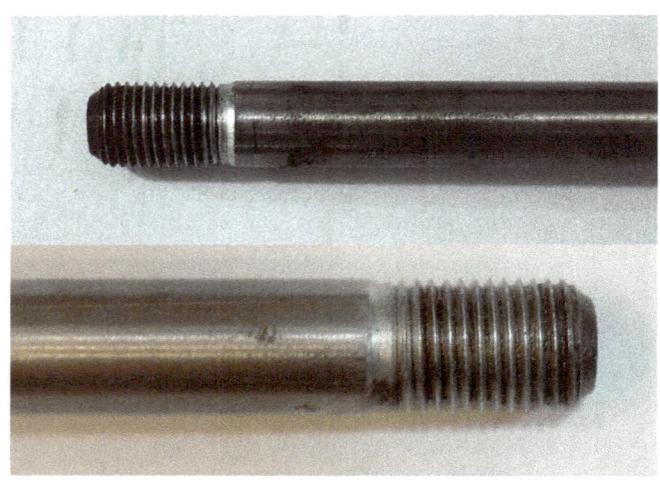

Top axle: Fine thread later production axle. Bottom axle: Coarse thread early production axle.

they made a comment about their test bike stating that they bent the right foot peg on their test ride. It is likely that if you find an early step bar today, chances are that it needs straightening.

Cylinder Head:

There are multiple versions of the cylinder heads. Engine number 100992 has "49cc" stamped into the cylinder head and engine number 100115 has M7 stamped into the head with no 49cc markings. These same features can be seen on K1s as well. The majority of '68 heads you will see have an "M" letter stamping on the shifter side of the head followed by a number.

Engine builder Tim Lavoi and Mini Trail guru Gary Lewis on separate occasions said that they have seen numerous stampings in Z50 cylinder heads and that only the early CT70's have a distinct marking on the silver tag heads.

The first 8,924 '68s or, all frames at or below frame serial number 108925, used a different camshaft than frames at serial number 108926 and beyond. The same Mini Trail frame numbers also used a different knock bolt to secure the cam sprocket to the camshaft. This change-over switched again at frame number 108926.

Engine Gaskets:

Original Z50A engines left the factory with black gaskets and seals. Many modern engine restorations have green, tan, brown, or light blue gaskets. If you are trying to restore your Mini Trail like it left the factory search for black engine gaskets.

Number 8 bolts & Hardware:

The '68 featured large number 8 stampings on the heads of the bolts used on this model. The most notable variations in number 8 bolts are found on the wheel rim dish bolts.

According to the Honda Parts book and the microfiche, all frames at 108925 and below used the large head bolts with washers. All others after frame number 108926 and above used flange bolts to fasten the rim dishes together.

The earlier serial number models like the slant guards featured standard head bolts and the later versions featured flange bolts. Standard head bolts can be found on frame number 100609 and 103147. Flange bolts can be found on frame numbers 108788, 109066, 116960 and 117234.

The bolt that clamps the muffler and head pipe together on frame numbers 100609 and 100896 both are in original patina and neither of them has a number "8" marking on the head of the bolt. This is the only bolt I have ever come across on the '68 that is not marked on the early production bikes.

Carburetor:

All '68 Z50s came with a simple carburetor with a hand lever choke. The unique feature on the '68 carburetors is the large knurled nut thumb screw to drain the gas out of the float bowl for easy transportation or storage. Also the bottom of the float bowl has a small removable drain. The carburetors came with black fuel line and clear drain line. Original Mini Trails will have drain line that is red from years of gas sitting in it. The fuel line is secured to the petcock with one metal clip and another clip on the carburetor outlet. One clip secures the overflow drain line to the bottom of the carburetor. The gas inlet pipe on the carburetor body is angled up instead of straight out.

Clutch Cover:

Use what you have left is often times the plan in the auto and motorcycle industry. This was certainly true for the '68. The oil clutch cover on some of the early serial number engines like number 100115, 100208, and 100992 used the cover that was left over from the 1967 Z50M. The text on the cover has distinct block style writing and the letter "L" is the letter to look for. When looking at the original '68 sales brochure you will not see the early cover. The brochure features a 68/69 style cover.

Another feature unique to the early style covers was the silver paint. The paint that was used on the early covers was very thin and not durable under high temperature situations. It is very common to see paint flaked off or burned off on the early style covers. This problem was corrected on the second generation covers. It is likely that if you find a later generation '68, no matter how bad of shape the bike is in, there is a very good chance the cover will not look as worn out as some of the low hour early '68s that have been well cared for.

Inside the clutch cover the oil pump body was changed to a different version after frame number

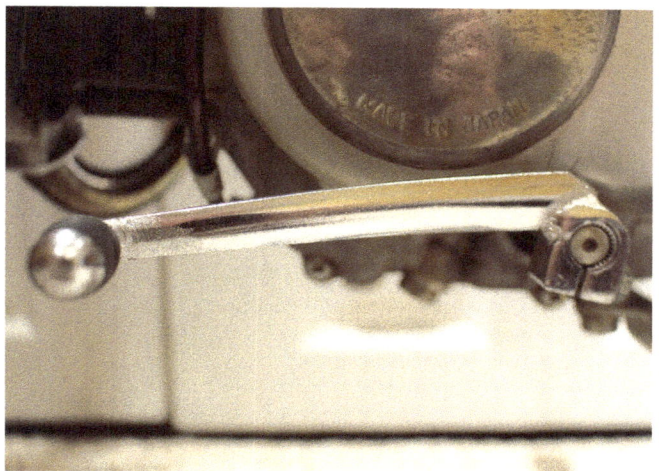

5-inch chrome gear shifter. Later switched to 5 ¼ inches for K1-K2 production.

Top picture: Kicker rubber lacking the "HM" logo. This version is found on both of my Tall Bar Mini Trails. Bottom picture: "HM" logo kicker rubber found on most Z50A's, all K1's, and K2's.

1968 Z50A Straight Guard in Bright Yellow/White-Ken Peare Collection.

1968 Honda Z50A Bright Yellow and White Slant Guard. Frame serial number 104332 and engine serial number 104443. Jeremy Polson Collection

1968 Honda Z50A Scarlet Red and White Slant Guard Saddleback Tall Bar. Frame Serial number 100896 and engine serial number 100208. Jeremy Polson Collection.

1968 Honda Z50A Scarlet Red and White Straight Guard. Frame serial number 109066 and engine number 108951. Jeremy Polson Collection.

108955. The early pump is part number 15311-035-000 and the later version is part number 15311-035-013 and was used on all engines at number 108956 and beyond.

Engine Cases:

All Z50As had two engines cases screwed together and sealed up with black gaskets to make up the transmission. What is unique about the '68 engine cases is that at the front of the block there is a distinct "lug" mark that sticks out. You will not see this on any other Z50 engine.

The clutch outer flywheel and the drive plate, just like a few parts in the cylinder head, switched over to a different version and part number at frame number 108926.

Axles and Axle Nuts:

According to the Honda parts manual, all '68s at and before serial number 108295 used a coarse thread front and rear axle with a 12mm self-locking nut. Frame number 108296 and into the end of K2 production used a fine thread and a matching 12mm self-locking nut. All '68s had zinc-plated front and rear axles with round heads on them.

Kicker and Shifter:

The kicker and shifter were both chrome plated parts. Both pieces had rubber to help eliminate slipping. Frame number 100609 and 100896 came with kickers that do not have "HM" stamped logos in the rubber, certainly a unique feature on these early serial number bikes. The "HM" logo is a common feature on-hardtail Mini Trails.

The shifter used on the '68s is a straight style shifter and the outer face of the shifter is slightly curved. The weld on the arm to the shaft indicates a down shift pattern. The shifter for the '68 is a different part number than the K1 and K2. The '68 shifters are slightly shorter in length than the later two models. It is so slight that it is only noticeable when matched up with a later style shifter, but there is a difference. All Z50 shifter rubbers do not have an "HM" logo stamped into them.

On the gear-shift drum, a contact fixing plate with part number 35755-001-020 was used up until frame number 103922 and all frames after that did not require this part.

'68 Paint Colors

As mentioned earlier, the '68 came in Bright

Yellow/White and Scarlet Red/White paint. Exactly how many of each color were made remains a mystery. Based on my research it appears that far fewer yellow models were produced than red ones. Yellow is the least produced out of the K1s and K2s as well.

Trying to figure out the pattern of paint production has been something of a struggle. Over the years I have pieced some information together and I will continue to plug information into the equation to try to unravel the mystery. I focused my attention on the tall bar serial number frames (101125 and below), but later started keeping a registry of all frame and engine numbers for the first year of the Z50A. I am always looking to add more to my list so don't hesitate to contact me with your information.

As of now I have come up with the following information. Serial number 100070 is documented red, Serial number 100128 documented red, 100217 documented yellow, 100502 documented red, 100609 documented red, 100645 documented red, 100659 documented red, 100720 painted red but no documentation, 100797 documented yellow, 100799 documented yellow, 100836 documented yellow, 100896 documented red, 100923 painted red but no documentation, 100965 documented red, 100992 documented red, 100996 documented yellow, 101016 documented yellow.

The '68 Z50A proved to be a success. If

1968 Honda Z50A Bright Yellow and White Straight Guard with a 7-seam seat...

...frame serial number 108788 and engine number 108858. Jeremy Polson Collection.

Note the Tall Bars, and the very rare 6-seam seat. The pride of my collection.

No one knows how many of these seats were used - but I consider this to be the Holy Grail of Z50s. Jeremy Polson Collection.

anything, it put Honda on the mini bike map. There was no way to predict how successful the next model was going to be especially when there were '68s still left over at some dealerships.

Holy Grail of Z50s

This bike is the only 6 seam seat '68 Mini Trail known to exist. The bike is also one of the early tall bars, with a saddle back frame, and a slant muffler protector. It is the lowest serial number Z50 in unrestored condition known to exist.

The bike is nicknamed "Jersey" as it was discovered by world famous Schwinn bike collector John Cellini of New Jersey. He purchased the bike in the late 1990's at the Mid-Ohio Motorcycle show. John and I connected in 2004 when I sold him an NOS front fork for the bike. The only major flaw on the bike is chipped paint on the front fork. The front fork was never switched and I still have it in the bag. It is frame number 100609, the 609th '68. 609 is a prominent area code in New Jersey, thus the nickname. Thanks to Gregg Davidian for selling me this rare piece of Honda history!

Chapter 2
1969-1970 Z50 K1

Engine serial number beginning and ending: Z50AE 120088 - 269999
Frame number beginning and ending: Z50A 120088 - 270235

In just six short months of sales the 1968 Z50A came and went, and Honda had bigger plans for its next model year.

The '68 was a primitive motorcycle, but certainly a step up from early factory built mini bikes. But it was the allure of the headlight and taillight that made the Z50A K1 appeal to so many people and by the time the K1 was released kids and adults alike were mini bike crazy!

In the summer of '69, Goldfines in my hometown of Duluth, Minnesota posted newspaper ads for a brand new 1968 Z50A on the showroom floor still for sale among a pile of brand new '69 K1s. With its price being so close to the K1 and a year old, it is no wonder why people passed up the '68 and went for the brand new K1. Side by side could you blame them? Especially with the hi/low headlight, taillight, battery, key ignition switch, front fork reflectors, and 3 all new color choices; 2 of which were candy colors!

In March of 1969 the Z50A K1 hit show room floors and the response was outstanding. By the end of production, a total of 150,147 Mini Trails were

141st K1 built, an early Candy Red cross over with leftover 1968 parts. Owned by author Jeremy Polson.

A Candy Blue Black Tag K1. The K1 on the cover is a Silver Tag. Both owned by author Jeremy Polson.

Black Tag K1 in Yellow. Owned by Author Jeremy Polson.

sold, making it one of the top selling motorcycles of all time. The Z50A line would go on to be American Honda's top selling model.

It is common for people to want to go back in time and pay the prices of that time period for their favorite childhood items. Exactly how much did a Z50A K1 cost you may ask? It depended on the area you lived in and how each dealer priced them. The suggested retail price for a K1 on the east coast was slightly higher because of the expense of shipping them across the country.

August 28th of 1969, Hurlbut Cycle Shop of Lincoln Nebraska purchased 16 Z50A K1s at $179.00 each. (The invoice is part of the Gary Lewis collection.) The suggested retail price was set at $245.00 plus delivery and set up. According to the 1970 Honda Price List that was confidential information for the dealers, the prices later in the model year went up to $184.00 on the West Coast and $186.10 on the east coast. Goldfines in my hometown of Duluth, Minnesota in August of 1970 was selling K1s as part of their "Back to Campus" sale for $229.00.

With this documentation it gives you an idea on the profit margin that dealers were working with. It is safe to say that between $50 and $100 was common profit on the Mini Trail K1s.

K1 sales ran from March of 1969 to June of 1970. With extensive research I have found that the end of the '68 Z50A production concluded in the month of December of 1968, and that the K1 was

  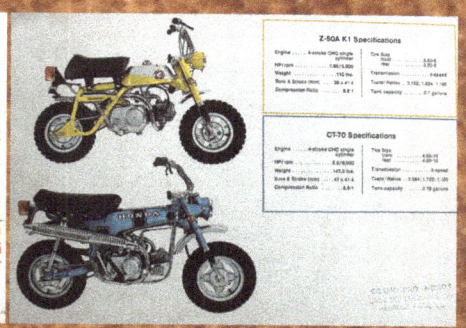

Z50A K1 Sales Brochure

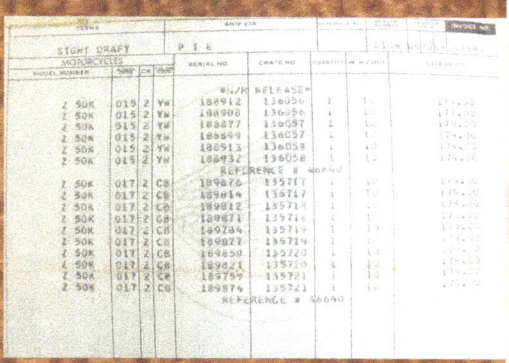  

An invoice to a Honda dealer from a Nebraska bank for 16 new Honda Z50A K1s. Gary Lewis Collection.

Handle grip hang tag Z50A K1

Every kid's dream - Win a Honda Mini - Duluth, Minnesota

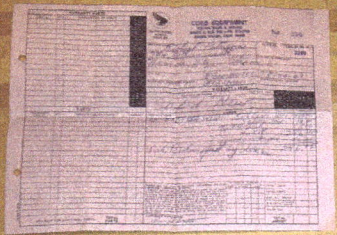    

Full Dealer Paperwork for an early K1

Realistic Mechanical Sound Effects Record Featuring Z50A K1

1970 Honda Dealer Price List

Honda Official Dealer Price List Showing What They Paid

Honda's Manufacturers Suggested List Prices (MSRP)

C-11H marked Z50A K1-K2 metal headlight bucket.

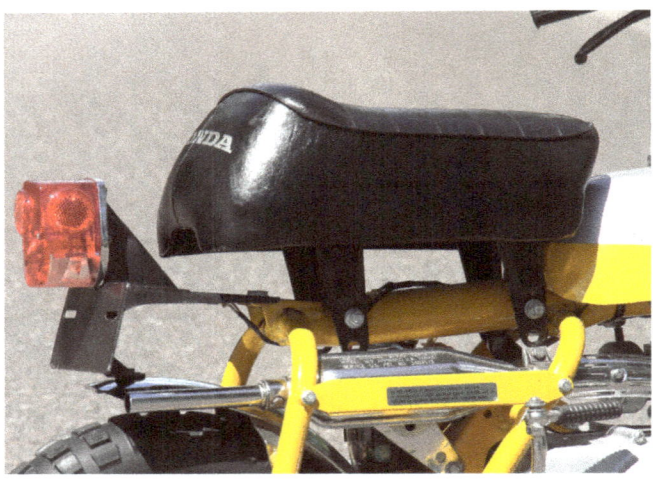

Razor edge thick center bracket chrome rear fender, K1 only. "Ski Jump" style rear frame tail light bracket mount found on later production K1s and all K2s

Early K1 small mounted "L" style rear frame tail light bracket mount found on early K1s

being built at the same time. Todd Thorson of Iowa and I both own December of 1968 built K1s. Scott Leach of California owns one of the final 1968 Z50As built; serial number 119351 or the 736th from the end of production. The build date on Scott's tank is December 26th 1968. K1 production ran from December of 1968 to December of 1969. With that being said Honda averaged 11,549 Z50's per month for the K1 production run.

To check the build dates of a frame or an engine you can look on the bottom of the tank under the area where the rubber pad mounts. You can also look on the frame on the backside of the rear chain adjustment ears and there most likely will be a build date. In my experience not all '68 tanks and frames have these numbers but all of the K1s I have seen have had these numbers. An example of a number code for a production date would be 81223 meaning 1968 December 23.

A Real Motorcycle:

In a sense the K1 was a mini motorcycle, and it was street legal. Not only did it have a headlight and taillight, it had a key switch ignition and a battery. It is these four features, along with the fact that this was the mini bike that most baby boomers grew up riding, that makes the Z50A K1 one of the most collectible Mini Trails today.

My dad and my uncle remember moving from an Arctic Cat mini bike to their blue/silver K1 in the spring of 1970. When I asked my dad how the Z50 compared he said, "The three speed transmission and the lighting made it head and shoulders better than the Arctic cat. It could climb hills like nothing and the Arctic Cat was slow".

All K1s came with a headlight, taillight, battery, a three position key ignition switch, a handlebar mounted high and low beam dimmer switch, chrome fenders and chain guard, black hand grips, gray cables with brake light switches, and chrome fold down handlebars.

The K1 and later the K2 would be the only Mini Trail models that came in three color options. All new for 1969 Honda gave the consumer the option to purchase a Candy Red/Silver, Candy Blue/Silver, or Bright Yellow/Silver Mini Trail.

As production went on there was a variation of the yellow/silver model. The later production color went from Bright Yellow, which was used on the '68 Z50A, to a mustard color yellow. The darkest shade of paint on the Candy Blue and Candy Red Z50s is usually along the bottom edges of the tank where the paint settled after the dipping process.

Candy colors vary depending on the temperature, the thickness of the paint, and how heavily the paint was applied. It is not uncommon to see several different shades of Candy Red and Candy Blue K1 colors based on the application of the paint as well as the fading of the paint over the years.

In some instances, it is common to see paint that is so sun faded that the silver base coat is the only paint remaining. It is also common to see painted components that have chipped or worn away over time and another color is underneath the paint because Honda used left over items when needed. I currently own a black tag candy blue/silver K1 and a Candy Ruby Red K2 and both have slight cable chafing on the sides of the headlight bucket with factory yellow paint underneath them. I have also seen candy red muffler protectors with paint chips in them

Front fork reflectors were added in 1969 to go with the headlight and taillight on the all new K1.

with Candy Blue paint underneath them.

Just like the 1968 Z50A, the 1969/70 Z50A K1 underwent many changes during production. And just like the Z50A, the easiest way to explain these variations is to break the motorcycle down part by part.

Frame

The K1 came in many frame variations. Many Mini Trail enthusiasts classify the K1 as either a "silver tag" Mini Trail or a "Black tag" Mini Trail. It is within these two models that the variations exist.

Silver Tags and Black Tags

The K1 was the first Mini Trail to feature a tag on the front steering head tube. The tag on the first production K1 Mini Trails came in silver with black text. The silver I.D. tags did not have a serial number or a date. The silver tag is adhered to the frame with an adhesive and not brass rivets like the black-tag models.

The silver tag is more common than most people think. K1 sales ran from March of 1969 to June of

Thin blade Z50A and Z50A K1 gas cap. K1 exclusive top of tank decal with 4 step battery removal instructions.

K1 exclusive black plastic hand brake levers. Used on frame number 254498 to 270235 or the last 15,537 frames.

The only Z50 to have a rectifier. Type II battery box with two mounting screws.

K1 ignition switch with 4 factory T-2 style keys. Early narrow steering fork stop.

1970. The silver tags are found on Mini Trails built prior to the release date of March 1969 up to the switch over to the black head tag, which began around September of 1969.

I currently own 6, K1s. I will use a silver tag and a black tag in Candy Blue and Silver in my collection to help you understand the production numbers on the I.D. tag variations. The serial number on the Silver tag bike is 173297 and the serial number on the September of '69 black tag is 217734. Out of the 150,147 K1s built, my September of '69 black tag is the 97,646th built.

A Candy Blue silver tag with frame number 199818 with a ski jump rear taillight mount and 5 chain adjuster marks on the rear of the frame sold on EBay in the spring of 2016. Let's suppose for a moment that this particular frame was the last silver tag produced. With that being said at least 79,730 silver tags would have been produced thus leaving 70,417 black tag models produced.

Based on my findings it leaves no question that there were more silver tags built than black tags. If you were hoping to sell your silver tag and you just read this, I hope I didn't ruin your auction description or your sales pitch. In reality though, the very early silver tags are among the rarest Mini Trails out there and I will help explain the variations.

The K1s built from September of 1969 with a black head tube tag and silver text featured a month and a year. A common example would be a 10/69 date code in the upper right hand corner of the steering head V.I.N tag. This format continued into the K2 model.

The silver tags are most recognized by the small taillight mount on the rear of the frame. It is not uncommon to see these early brackets broken off. However, not all silver tags had the small style taillight bracket. The taillight mounts on the rear of the frame switched from the basic "L" shaped bracket somewhere in the month of August of 1969 between frame numbers 187970 and 198198.

Early models have a narrow steering stop like the '68. Later versions featured a tab that started wider at the top and got narrower towards the bottom. The ignition switch mount has been spotted in at least two different versions on the silver tag and one style on the black tag.

Type 1: It features a '68 style welded seam mounted ignition bracket with a back stop tab like the one found on Todd Thorson's early K1, the 208th made.

Type II: It features the welded seam ignition mount but this version does not have the tab.

Type III: It features a spot-welded bracket and no tab.

Crossover Models:

One of the most difficult things to document and figure out about the K1s are the cross over variations. When exactly did the '68 parts/design features run out? And when were the Mini Trails produced that featured all of the "new" K1 parts?

Over the years several skeptics have argued that no '68 parts came on K1s and that Honda would not build bikes like that. Perhaps one of my all-time favorite discoveries is an original 1969 Candy Blue/Silver gas tank with a welded fuel neck left over from the '68s and used on frame number 1024988, the 4,900th K1 made. This tank currently is part of my collection.

K1-K2 handlebar assembly with grommet holes facing the rider. Early K1's used a different set of bars. See handlebar section.

Side reflector Stanley taillight lens used K1-K2. Straight muffler diffuser, K1 exclusive. Small mounting bracket K1 exclusive taillight bracket.

This isn't the only Mini Trail like this. As mentioned earlier Todd Thorson of Jewell, Iowa owns a very early K1. His frame number is 120296, the 208th K1 produced. The engine is 120092, the 4th K1 engine in the serial number sequence. The first K1s produced were Candy Red/Silver.

There are several parts that are found on the silver tag Mini Trails that have a resemblance to the '68. Many early silver tags came with the long tail flywheel cover. There are some silver tags that have been spotted with leftover patent pending mufflers with the straight stinger. There are also many silver tags that came with mufflers that have the patent numbers on the mufflers; however, they feature the notch like cut out in the rear of the muffler like the '68 to lock the stinger in place. Also, 415 chains and sprockets are commonly found on the cross over K1s.

Right side handlebars with side-mounted holes in them for the throttle cable outlet are present on early silver tag models. The left handlebar on the early silver tags had the dimmer switch wire exit out of the bottom portion of the bar instead of the backside that faces the rider. Non-reinforced seat pans left over from the '68s were used on early K1s as well.

There are two battery boxes that exist on the K1 and certainly type I battery boxes are present on the early silver tags. Clear muffler protector decals like the ones used on the '68 were used on the early yellow K1s. There have been some K1s spotted with type III style 7 seam '68 seats and '68 engine serial numbers. Mark Mitchell of California purchased a K1 with a 19,222 series engine on it which technically is a left over engine from a 1968. The frame number on this particular bike is 120229. It is the 141st K1 produced. I purchased this Mini Trail from Mark in the winter of 2015. Both Todd Thorson and I have left over '68 seats on our early K1s. Our bikes are 67 serial numbers apart.

Left to right: Yuasa B60-6 replacement battery. B60-6 Yuasa "winged" Honda battery, the type installed at the factory. Jeremy Polson Collection

Cloud Silver wheels with flange bolts used on all K1 models.

Headlight Assembly:

All K1s came with a headlight that featured a high and low beam bulb inside. The outer casing was painted to match the frame and it featured a chrome trim ring, a hi/low beam red jewel indicator, and a flat piece metal emblem with a chrome edge, red main section, and a white "H" in the center to represent Honda. The emblem was used to cover the hole in the top of the bucket since no speedometer was used on the U.S. model. The back of the headlight bucket was plugged with a small black flat rubber plug also known as the "useless hole plug". The hole in the back of the bucket was intended for a speedometer cable.

There are plastic and metal reproduction buckets available. But it doesn't stop there. Some people try to pass off metal PC50 or P50 buckets with the flat spot in the backside as K1-K2 buckets. The number one thing to look for on an original bucket is the "C-11H" marking on the kicker side of the bucket. The marking is stamped into the metal.

Taillight Assembly:

All K1 frames came with a taillight mounting bracket on the rear of the frame to house the taillight assembly. The bracket came in a semi-gloss paint and it had a small license plate frame on it. The taillight bracket had a straight support piece compared to the K2 version which curved up in the back where it mounts to the frame. The lower portion of the bracket that mounts to the rear fender requires a rubber grommet, metal insert sleeve, and a mounting bolt. This portion of the bracket is much smaller than the K2 version.

Current reproduction taillight brackets have flooded the market. They are laser cut and have modern manufacturing spot welds so they are easily distinguished from the originals.

Handlebars:

With the addition of the headlight and taillight on the K1 model, the left hand bar was outfitted with a hi/low beam black dimmer switch with a gray casing. The dimmer switch on/off switch is mounted to the assembly with two small Phillips head screws. Current issue Honda versions of the switch are attached by snapping the switch into place and it comes with a black sheathing. Parts suppliers have converted the new issue switch with new gray sheathing so beware of the snap on on/off switch if they claim it is NOS.

Two left handlebars exist for the K1. The first bar has a hole drilled next to the hand grip for the dimmer switch to mount and the other hole is in the outer bottom corner of the bar for the dimmer switch wires to exit out so they can plug into the headlight and wire harness. This handlebar has been spotted on frame number 141611 or the 21,523rd K1 produced.

The second version of the left bar has the same upper hole next to the grip, however this time the dimmer switch exits out the backside of the bar and faces the rider when seated on the motorcycle.

The "use what you have mentality" stuck around for many silver tag models. Honda continued to use the right side bar with the side mounted throttle hole that was plugged with a black rubber grommet from the '68. How many silver tags used the '68 right side handlebar? I will put things in perspective. More K1s used it than there were '68s built. I own an original parts bike with frame number 148529. With that being said, if that was the last silver tag that featured that bar it would put the total at over 28,441st produced, far surpassing '68 production totals.

I own silver tag number 173297 or the 53,209th K1 and it does not have the side mount throttle cable hole, or the bottom hole left side handlebar. The new design for the right side bar had the throttle cable hole come out the backside to match the exit hole on the left side handlebar.

Front Fender:

All silver tags as well as early black tags came with the '68 style short front fender in chrome with no cable notch in the side. One thing to keep in mind is that the K1 fender is shorter than the '68 front fender. Some restorers try to use K1 fenders on the '68 thinking that by painting it up it will get the job done. As production went on Honda made a design change to the front fender adding a right side curved notch in it to allow the front brake cable to slide alongside it. The new design feature served two purposes. The first was that it made room for the front brake cable and stopped it from rubbing a groove in the side of the fender. Secondly it kept the cable from wearing out.

The type I fender without the notch is present on frame number 240425 or the 120,337th K1. The type II fender with the notch is present on frame number 244702 or the 124,614th K1.

Rear Fender:

Like the front fender the rear fender on the K1 came in chrome. The center mounting bracket unlike the '68 was large and in charge. It was a solid mounted bracket with 8 spot welds. The center spot welds

35 tooth rear sprocket. 415 chains used on early models and 420s used on the majority of K1-K2 models. Early K1s used up left over Z50A chains and sprockets. Note the short tail flywheel cover used on majority of K1s and all K2s.

Z50A and early K1 long tail flywheel cover.

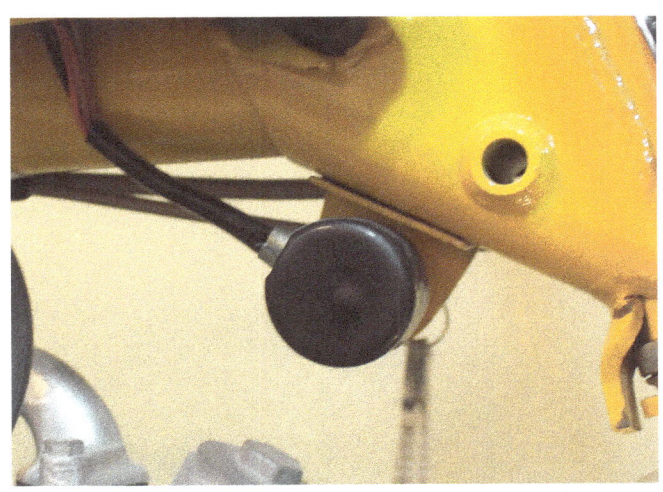

Dimple back ignition switch used on some late K1s - a vendor variation part. Wider steering fork stop found on late K1s and all K2s.

A later K1 razor edge chrome front fender with a cable guide notch.

An early K1 razor edge chrome front fender without a cable guide notch.

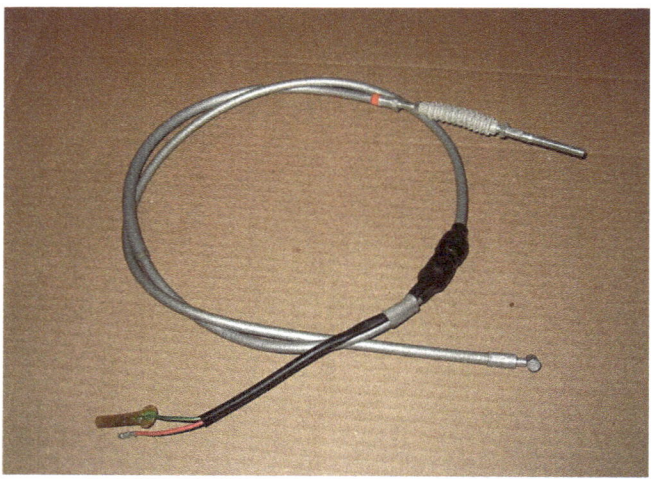

New Old Stock Z50A K1 cable with integrated brake light switch. The cables are silver/Gray with T.S.K made in Japan markings.

dimple the fender and give it a dented look. The rear edge of the fender has a sharp edge like the '68. This would later be changed to a rolled edge on the K2 for safety reasons.

Chain Guard

The K1 brought back the look of the 1967 Z50M with a chain guard. This time it was chrome to match the all new fender design. The lower mounting tab on the chain guard is skinny in nature and often times is cracked or broken.

Two versions of the chain guard exist. The early model bikes have a bend/crease in the lower mounting tab and the later ones had a flat lower mounting tab.

Brake Cables

Like the '68, the K1 came with TSK made in Japan silver/gray brake cables. Being that the Mini Trail came with lights, the cables were outfitted with front and rear brake light switches. There are multiple versions of the brake cables when it comes to originality and restorations. The original cables came with small metal ends that mounted into the brake levers and later on they were switched to a larger end knob.

Honda produced black brake cables as service replacement parts and though they are factory made parts they were never installed on factory built K1s.

Today there are Chinese made cables that have red bands on them to match the new old stock replacement cables Honda sold over the years. And like the new old stock cables the red bands did not come on the cables from the factory on this model Z50. Stamped part numbers in the cable casings are common among all cables that did not come on factory produced Mini Trails as well.

Chain/Rear Sprocket/Front Sprocket:

Just like the later '68s the K1s used 12 tooth front drive sprockets with a 35 tooth rear sprocket. As of January of 1969, the Honda Book II parts source shows all K1s requiring a 74 link 420 chain.

However, as mentioned earlier, 415 chains and 35 tooth sprockets have been found on earlier K1s. My Candy Red/Silver K1; the 141st off the line, as well as Todd Thorson's early K1, are great examples of this.

Ignition key switch:

Gone are the basic on/off toggle switches for the '69 K1 model. The K1 featured a three position key switch with a direct plastic plug to harness set up. The ignition switch was serial number coded to match the code on the small Honda wing keys that came with the Mini Trail. When the K1s left the factory they came with four keys on a small chrome key ring.

Some Mini Trails came with 4 keys and some only came with 2 keys. The reason for the different quantities of keys is because some dealers kept the backup keys in case you lost your keys. You could stop in and ask for a replacement and they would sell you your old keys. Gary Lewis and Mark Troxell at Honda Keys.com own thousands of leftover dealer keys.

Two different plug connectors have been spotted on the K1. A clear plug connector on early models that looks like the connector on the Z50M and a white plug connector, which is the most common. The clear plug connector has been spotted on various bikes in the first 10,000 or so K1s produced.

Battery Box/strap/& Battery:

A new feature for 1969 was the addition of a battery. All K1s came with a clear overflow tube. The original batteries that came from the factory had a yellow Honda wing on the front. Two NOS green versions exist; the original style winged version and a non-winged version. There are modern versions of the battery floating around in white as well as off brand green batteries with red tops and black tops. Some restorers try and fool people with a 6N2A-2C green battery on their restorations so beware of those as well.

Being that the earliest silver tag frames had a different battery box mounting set up, they required the Type I battery box. All frames from 102088 up to frame number 1028646 fell into the type I frame and battery box category according to the Honda parts books. However, I have owned a couple bikes with early battery boxes over 1,000 serial numbers higher than what the parts book claims. The type I battery box required four 5x16 mm pan screws and four plain 5mm washers to secure the battery box to the frame.

All frames and battery boxes from 1028647 up to frame number 270235 fell into the Type II category. The type II battery box required two 5x45 mm pan screws and two 5mm plain washers. Type II frames and battery boxes are found on both silver tag and black tag models.

To secure the battery to the battery box, all K1s used a rubber strap with zinc plated ends. The new issue straps that are available from Honda have gold colored metal ends and some are found with silver ends. The main difference between the original battery

Early K1 chain guard with a factory bend at the top of the lower mounting bracket. Later brackets were straight.

"HM" stamped foot peg rubber Z50A-Z50A K2.

An original factory welded neck Candy Blue/Silver tank found on one of the 1st 5,000 K1's built. Jeremy Polson Collection.

Nitto Brand tires, double nutted brass valve stem nuts, and Cloud Silver painted wheels.

The lowest production tire used on the Z50 Mini Trail was the Yokohama brand tire.

Bridgestone brand tires were used on the earliest K1s as well as many other K1s. The 141st K1 came with Bridgestone tires.

strap and the current issue is the originals have a smooth texture and the new issue straps have a pimple texture and mold marks.

Gas Tank:

The K1 gas tanks like most of the '68 tanks were dipped at the factory. This time the only difference was that candy paint was used on the red and the blue tanks. As mentioned earlier, the yellow remained the same and actually came in bright yellow to start with and was later changed to a more mustard shade of yellow. The tanks were painted silver first and then dipped in either candy tone red or blue or either shade of yellow. The most noticeable color difference is along the bottom edges of the candy painted tanks because that is where the paint all runs to when it is pulled out of the paint trough. The bottoms of the tanks have a paddle mark just like most '68 tanks.

The front bottom of the tank has two mounting spots and the rear has a mounting peg. The rear peg requires a rubber banding strap to secure the tank to the back bone. The front of the tank slides onto two small flat metal tabs that are covered with two tank cushions that had small slits in the backsides to slide smoothly onto the tank cushions. All frames at serial number 173239 required the early style front tank cushions. Later in production the flat metal tabs were changed to small rods welded into the frame and they required front tank cushions with holes in the backsides. All frames at 173240 and through the end of the K2 production required the front tank cushion that had small holes in the backside of them to push smoothly onto the frame rods.

The rear of the tank also has a rubber cushion that pushes into the bottom of the tank to hold it and it allows the tank to sit firmly on the backbone without scratching the paint or sliding around.

Emblems:

Just like the '68, the K1 came with the same round badge on each side of the tank that said "Honda" on top and "Mini Trail" on the bottom with the signature wing in the center. The badges were chrome, red, and white, with black letters. The badges were secured to the tank with two chrome headed Phillips head 3mm screws. The screws had a dot punch mark in them. The modern replacement screws have a dot mark and a plus mark.

Tires:

You didn't have your choice of tires on the K1, but that doesn't mean that only one tire was used.

Honda took advantage of multiple vendors in order to produce over 150,000 Mini Trails in a short amount of time. It is very common to see Bridgestone tires on K1s, however Nitto tires are found on both silver tag and black tag bikes. Yokohama tires were also found on silver tag and black tag bikes. The 141st and 208th K1s produced came with Bridgestone tires.

Wheels & Bolts:

All K1s came with four round hole style wheels in Cloud Silver paint like the '68s. The wheels were held together by Honda's grade eight zinc coated flange wheel bolts. The number 8 markings changed through the production run. The wheel bolts were marked with gold, black, or blue paint for torque specs.

Hubs

All K1s came with 4 bolt pattern mounted aluminum hubs with a light clear coat on them. It is very common to see the clear coat yellowed on original hubs and or flaked or chipped up. The hubs are mounted on the two piece wheels with large number-eight grade-marked bolts with spring washers coated in zinc.

Two versions of the rear hub exist on the K1. The early style rear hub has rounded sprocket mounting bolt tubes and the later style rear hub has flat machined sections in each of the three bolt tubes. The later style hub would carry over to the K2 model.

Foot pegs & step bar:

All K1s came with a sturdy foot peg bar, a design that was later changed during the '68 production model year. The foot peg pillions are also double reinforced for added strength. The peg rubbers are black and feature the signature "HM" logo. The foot pegs are fastened to the bottom of the engine with four marked-eight zinc coated bolts with spring washers.

Handbrake levers:

Two sets of handbrake levers were used on the K1. All silver tag models and most black tag models came with black plastic levers. The parts books show that the switch to aluminum levers took place at frame number 254499. That means that the final 15,737 units out of 150,147 had aluminum levers.

Petcock

Bikes at serial number 1242186 and below used the 1968 style petcock. Bikes at 12421187 and above used the new version found on the K2.

A K1 exclusive 6 seam smooth grain split seam vinyl seat.

A later production K1 seat pan with gusset plates welded to the seat pan for added strength.

A K1 carburetor with a small drain screw and non-recessed air and idle screws. Also used on early K2s.

A left over Pat. Pend muffler from the Z50A. This was found on the 141st K1-Jeremy Polson Collection.

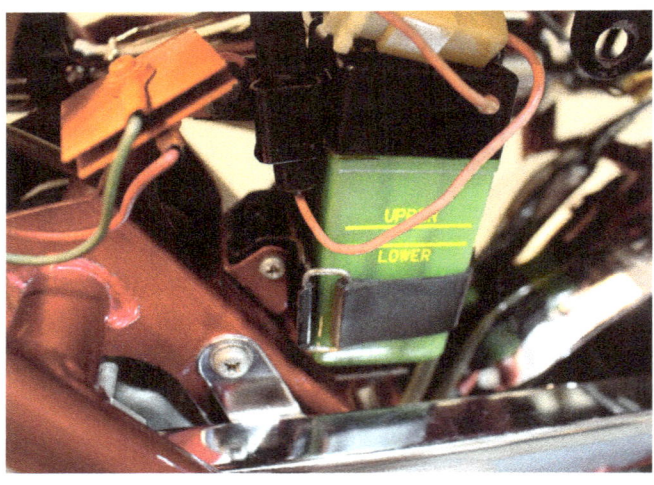

Above: Early K1 battery box with 4 pan head screws to mount it to the frame.

Top Right:
1969 Silver Tag K1 Identification tag.

Lower Right:
1970 Black Tag Identification tag. 1970 model year bikes started with bikes built in September of 1969.

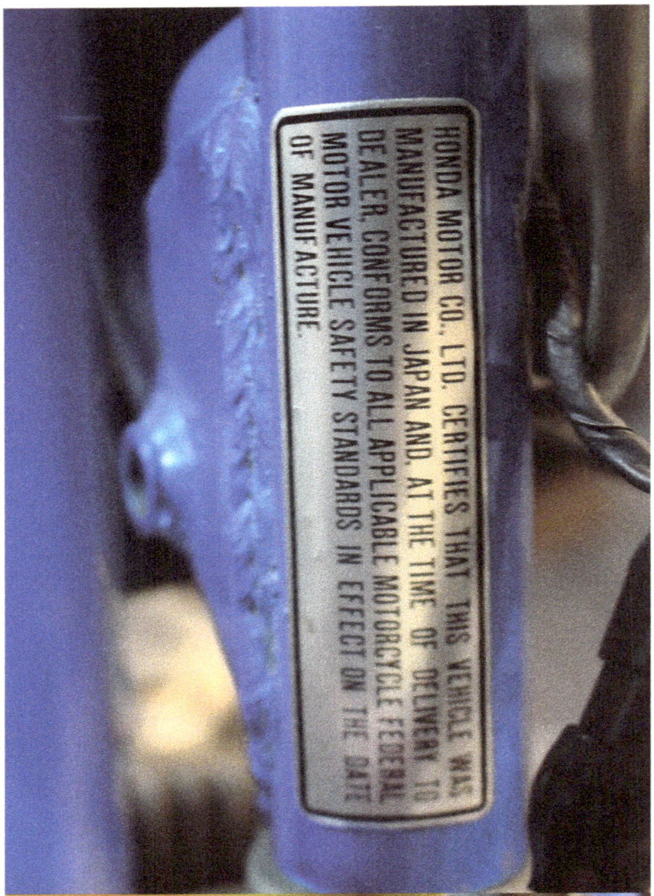

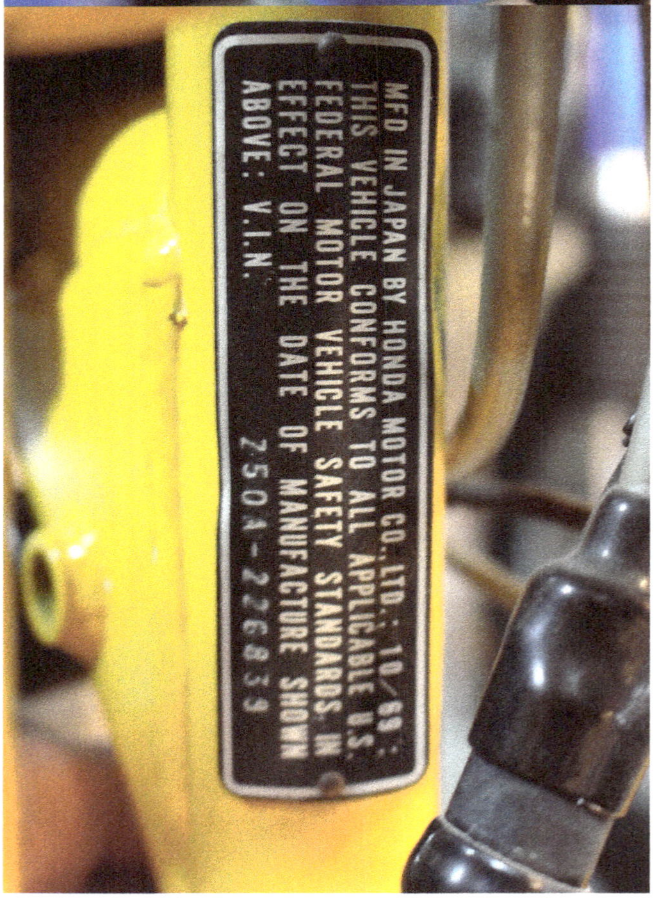

Chapter 3
1970-1971 Z50 K2

Engine serial number beginning and ending: Z50AE 270236 - 999999
Frame number beginning and ending: Z50A 270236 - 387884

The K1 was a huge success and the all new K2 was ready to follow in its footsteps. K2 production began just after the New Year in 1970 and actually ran until April of 1972.

Two January of 1970 I.D. serial numbers were given to me in a small registry. The frame serial numbers are Z50A 270718, the 482nd K2 built and serial number 273220, the 2,984th K2 built. The highest serial number K2 I had on registry for years was frame serial number 379244, the 109,008th K2 built and it was built in April of 1972.

Then in 2015 Jesse Kimball of Grand Marais, Minnesota, about 2 hours north of me, sent me frame numbers 387072 & 387640. Both are Candy Ruby Red and both are April of 1972 V.I.N tags. The higher serial number is the 117,404th out of 117,648 made. Jesse still owns these rare bikes.

I currently own serial number Z50A 279149, the 8,913th K2 built. The I.D. head tag on this particular Ruby Red Mini Trail says that it

Candy Sapphire Blue/White fuel tank with silver decals with black text.

Mexican Yellow/White fuel tank with silver decals with black text. K2 exclusive oval tank emblems.

Candy Ruby Red/White fuel tank with clear decals with silver text.

was built in February of 1970. The K2 became available for sale on July 1st of 1970. In total 117,648 K2s were sold. The interesting part about both of Jesse's K2s is that the engine numbers are higher than the highest production K2 frame made. His serial numbers are 403731 & 404480.

At a glance, if your eye were to spot the long rear fender, the foot brake, or the oval tank badge, one might think the K2 is almost the same bike as the K1 but in reality almost every part is different in some subtle way.

The tank badges are what most people commonly refer to as the "oval badges" and they are one of many changes for the K2 model. The badges are chrome with the word Honda also in chrome and Mini Trail in a black "70s" style text outlined in chrome. They have an orange background with black oval outline around the badge.

The gas tank shape remained the same as the Z50A and Z50A K1; however, the paint scheme was switched around putting the primary frame color up top and the secondary color on the bottom.

The K2 came in Candy Sapphire Blue, Candy Ruby Red, and Mexican Yellow as the primary colors and white as the secondary color.

The tank decal design changed from the previous two years in many ways. First of all, it went from one decal to two. Next it came in either clear with silver text or silver with black text. The interesting thing about both versions is that they are not the exact same decals in different colors but rather completely different decals. It did not matter if the bike was an early or later production bike as both styles have been found on early and late run bikes.

Like the later K1s, the K2 frames had round stock gas tank mounting tabs and used the round rubber gas tank mounts up front and the rubber tank pad and strap in the rear.

The petcock valve was the larger oval style petcock and not the simple butterfly design like the Z50A and the earlier Z50A K1 had. The petcock filter was tan and this time came in plastic. The modern version comes in a baby blue color.

The gas cap was changed slightly for the K2 model. The on/off butterfly instead of being straight and simple was changed slightly to one with rounded corners. This design would stick around until the end of the Z50A run in 1978.

For safety reasons as well as functionality the fenders were redesigned in a couple of ways. For safety reasons they had rolled edges instead of razor edges. The center front fender mounting bracket was wider and sturdier than the simple spot welded or riveted fenders on the Z50A and Z50A K1. The front and rear fenders were also much longer than the previous two model years.

The long rear fender required a longer taillight bracket so it was changed to fit the newly designed rear fender. The K2 taillight bracket was also structurally stronger than the K1 bracket. The K2 was the last Mini Trail to use the dual sided reflector Stanley taillight lens. All K2 frames came with the later K1 style "ski jump" taillight bracket mount on the rear of the frame.

At a glance one might think the seat is the same as the K1 until the rider steps off and reveals the very durable "pebble grain" top seat cushion. The rear of the seat remained the same with the split seam and the Honda logo stenciled on in silver text. The tool kit clips were switched from a wire clip to a humped solid metal clip. The tool kit was a single sided plug wrench and bar. Just like the end of the K1 production run, the K2 came with black tipped aluminum brake levers.

The electrical system was changed up on the K2 in a number of ways. The ignition switch added a white wire and this time the back rubber water cover had a dimple in the center of the cover on the later versions of the switch. The cover was shiny rubber compared to the matte finish rubber cover on the K1 and early K2s. The wire harness was changed in a few ways as well. In order to connect the redesigned ignition, another connector had to be added to the harness. Being that the K2 did not have a battery, the battery plug connector was eliminated. The lights ran off the newly redesigned stator and magneto assembly. The ignition coil changed as well and this time came in gray instead of a marble finish.

Late K1-K2 petcock fuel valve. 2nd run K2 carburetor with a recessed air screw. Early K2's used left over K1 carburetors until they were used up.

K2 exclusive long style chrome front fender with rolled safety edges.

An early K2 chain guard. The lower mounting bracket is slightly wider than the late K1 chain guard.

35 tooth rear sprocket combined with a 74 link 420 chain.

K2 exclusive sturdier taillight bracket and long rear fender with rolled safety edges and sturdy center mounting bracket.

K2 exclusive "Pebble Grain" seat with a split seam in the rear of the seat.

The spark plug cap was a Honda "HM" logo cap. The dimmer switch remained the same as the K1. However, the difference for the K2 is that when Honda mounted them at the factory they wrapped the dimmer switch casing around the rear brake cable.

The headlight bucket for the most part remained the same. The only change was the light case emblem. Instead of the large "H" like the K1 had, it was switched up to the word "Honda". Honda is in chrome text with a black background and a white circle border.

The exhaust system saw several changes from end to end. The head pipe remained the same; however, this time it featured a louvered lower heat shield. The muffler had a significant stamping in the upper right hand corner that read "HM045". This muffler was added later in the K2 run. I own an early K2 with a left over K1 muffler that does not have the HM045 stamping; however, it does have the K2 stinger. The stinger was changed from a straight style to a slightly curved end to get away from the rear fender. The band clamp remained the same; the only difference was on the K2 it was mounted flat so it was clear from the seat post.

The handlebar assembly on the K2 was identical to the later K1 bar assembly from the triple clamp, nuts, twist knobs, and bars with the cable holes facing the rider and plugged with black rubber grommets. Just like the K1, the K2 had black rubber grips.

The K2 used a different paint code for the wheels. The part number instead of ending in 670 AU like the Z50A and Z50A K1, the K2 used a 670 S part number. The problem with the original K2 wheels is that the paint was a bit thinner silver and did not hold up as well as the earlier wheels. It is very common to see K2s in nice condition with rusty wheel dishes.

Just like the rest of the hardware on the K2 the "pig nosed" bolts were used. The purist who wants to restore their K2 the way it came from the factory needs to pay attention to the wheel bolt mounting pattern. The front wheel has the flange bolt heads facing out on the kicker side of

Candy Sapphire Blue Z50A K2 owned by Author Jeremy Polson.

First year for the rear foot brake pedal assembly. K2 exclusive louvered lower heat shield.

An early Candy Ruby Red K2 with a left over K1 muffler.

HM045 stamped muffler used on all but the early production K2's. A new muffler protector decal with black line above and below the text was added for the K2 model.

the motorcycle and the nuts and washers are on the shifter side. On the rear wheel the nuts are on the kicker side and the flange bolt heads are on the shifter side. This subtle detail is evident in the sales brochure and when examining original motorcycles. Many restorations lack this subtle detail, it started with the K1 black tags.

When it comes to tire brands the K2 used a variety. The following brands have been found on them: Bridgestone, Bridgestone Trail Wing 2, Nitto, and Yokohama.

The K2 used the later style K1 rear hub with the flat grind sections on the hub shaft. The hub took a 35 tooth rear sprocket and was secured with 3 bolts and a tongue washer. The bike was driven with a 74 link 420 chain.

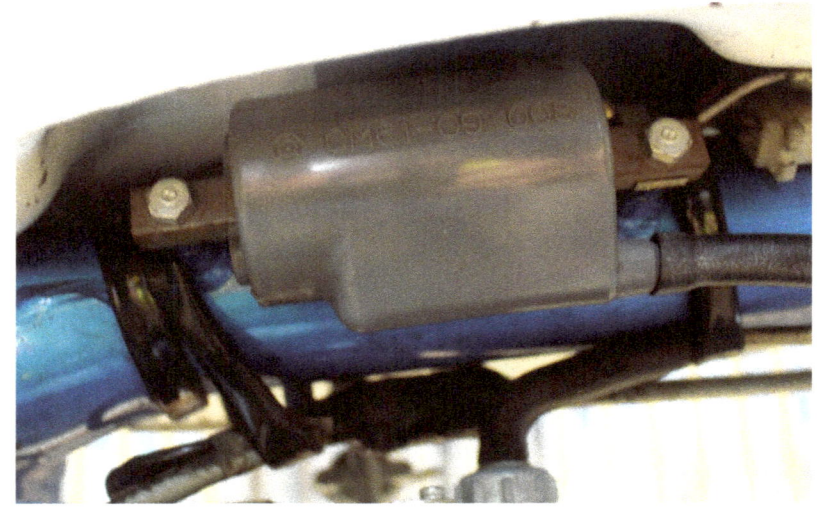

A K2 exclusive solid dark gray coil.

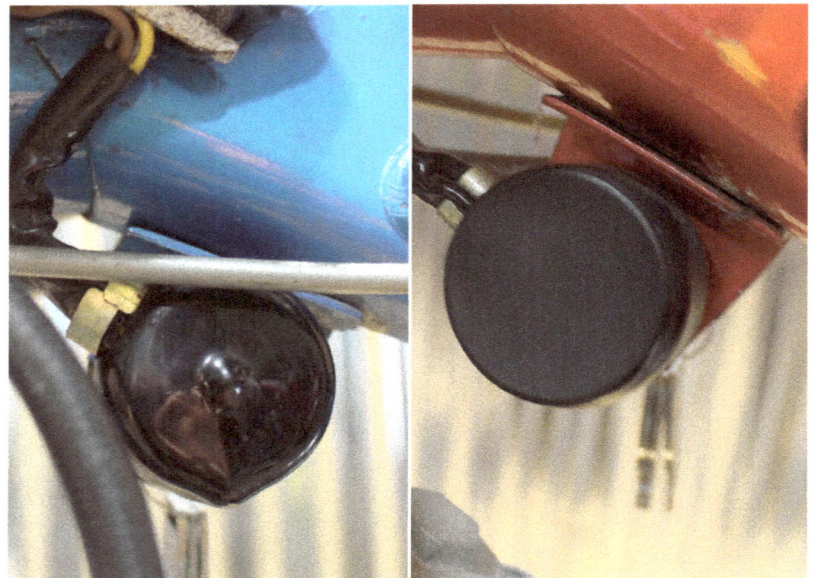

*Left: A dimple back ignition switch cover found on most K2 models.
Jeremy Polson Collection.*

*Right: Early K2 ignition switch cover found on the 8,913th K2 built.
Jeremy Polson Collection.*

To cover the chain, the K2 had an all-chrome chain guard. The chain guard was improved over the previous model in the lower mounting tab with a wider tab. The beginning of the K2 run featured a chain guard that had a slightly wider lower bracket than the K1 and later in the run it was switched to the well-known wider mounting bracket or "Fat bracket".

The number one thing to look for when searching for an original K2 engine is to make sure it has the rear brake cable tab mounted behind the top oil cover case screw to keep the cable tucked behind the frame. This part is an exclusive K2 part because of the foot brake assembly and often times is missing when the engine cover has been removed.

One of the most recognizable parts on the K2 is the foot brake pedal; a safety feature that would remain on all Z50's. All new for the K2 was a chrome plated foot pedal assembly. The rear brake cable was mounted into a slide assembly and when the rider pressed down on the pedal or pulled on the lever the slide would pull the rod and spread the brake shoes.

To go with the foot pedal and rear brake cable a frame mounted bracket was added to the K2 to house a taillight brake switch. The brake switch casing came in gray to match the cables. A modern version is floating around as a replacement part and has black casing. In order to make the foot brake function, a rear brake slide was attached to the pedal and a rod was attached to the rear hub brake arm. This is a complex system and is only used on the Z50A K2. All K2s used the short style flywheel cover that replaced the long tail cover on the K1.

Once the 2nd run of the triple clamp was replaced on the K1, a multiple bracing clamp was used and it was used entirely on the K2. Once the K1 style carburetors ran out, a redesigned carburetor came out during the K2 production run. This carburetor had the small drain knob like the K1, however it had a recessed air screw.

New solid metal tool kit clips replaced the wire clips used on the Z50A and Z50A K1.

A K2 exclusive rear fender guide tab. This mounted to the top engine oil cover screw to hold the cable in place. NOS clips courtesy of the Gary Lewis Collection.

Round louvered 2-piece air cleaner Z50A-K2. Short tail flywheel covers late K1-K2.

Reinforced gusset braced triple clamp, later K1-K2. New Old Stock, Gary Lewis Collection.

K2 exclusive headlight badge with "Honda" wording.

Black grips, K1-K2. Aluminum hand brake levers, last 15,537 K1s and all K2s.

Mexican Yellow Honda Z50A K2 owned by Author Jeremy Polson.

Yellow is the lowest production color in the Z50A Hard Tail series. Type II wide lower mounting bracket chain guard. Used on most K2 models.

Candy Sapphire Blue Honda Z50A K2. The dimmer switch wire was wrapped around rear brake cable from the Factory-Jeremy Polson Collection.

Candy Ruby Red Honda Z50A K2 owned by Author Jeremy Polson.

C-11H metal headlight bucket in Mexican Yellow.

Candy Sapphire Blue Honda Z50A K2 owned by Author Jeremy Polson.

Honda Shocks the Mini Bike World!

The Era of the Soft Tail Begins!

Chapter 4
1972 Z50A K3

Engine beginning and ending serial numbers: 1000001 - 29999999
Frame beginning and ending serial numbers: 1000001 - NA
Carburetor serial number: 655 A

The First Soft Tail
On January 1st 1972 Honda released the first Z50A soft tail model, the K3. The rear shock design would last until the final Z50 rolled off the assembly line in 1999. The first soft tail model came in two color choices: Light Ruby Red/Black and Candy Gold/Black.

This model was the first to have a seat that featured chrome side buttons like the CT70. The seat top had a smooth grid and box pattern design which was different than the hardtails' straight rib pattern and featured a stenciled Honda logo on the rear in silver. The top grain was similar to the Z50A and K1 style and not at all like the pebble grain seat top on the K2. Although this new seat design would last until the end of the 1978 production, this particular seat was only used on the K3.

The seat pan featured short mounting legs when compared to the hardtails, so there was no

Candy Gold/Black K3.

All new 1-piece exhaust system with chrome upper and lower heat shields.

clearance underneath for a tool kit.

Instead of tool clips under the seat, a plastic side cover painted to match the tank was installed on the shifter side of the Mini Trail to house the tool kit. This design concept was a carryover from earlier hardtail Japanese domestic models. Underneath the cover was a plastic tool kit holder mounted to the frame for the spark plug wrench and bar. The K3 side cover did not feature any "Z50" decals but rather just a clear transporting instructional decal with black text on the candy gold cover and silver text on the light Ruby Red cover.

The K3 had a 7-digit frame serial number unlike the previous models that only had 6 digits. Engines were still 6 digits. The rear fender did not have an extra oval shaped stamped hole in it nor was it plugged with a black rubber plug. That version of the fender did not come into production until the 1975 K6. The extra hole found on later fenders is for a different style taillight bracket thus making the later style fender universal for several models. The rear fender came with a black tire pressure decal with silver text. In the upper right hand corner of the decal it said Z50A K3.

The unique feature about the chrome front fender was the bottom - it came with a reinforcement plate welded in place with two captured nuts so when the mounting bolts went in from the top they were secured by the bottom nuts like the hardtail fenders. This style fender was used on the K3, K4, and K5 models. The fender, like the K2, had the rolled-under safety edges.

New for '72 was a larger one-piece exhaust system. The exhaust pipe came in flat black with a curved flat black stinger, two chrome lower heat shields, and a large chrome upper heat shield. The newly designed black curved diffuser would be used on the K3, K4, and K5 models before undergoing another change.

To match the chrome heat shields, the units were outfitted with front and rear chrome fenders, rear shocks, bars, chain guard, gas cap, and foot pedal.

The K3 would be the last Mini Trail to feature a chrome chain guard with the exception of some of the earliest K4's. The unique feature about the chain guard is the little clear vibration plug in the bottom back corner of it. This is one of those details you look for when checking the originality of a Mini Trail or a proper restoration.

The handle bars, like those on the hardtail, were chrome but they had a two-piece high rise triple clamp, more aggressive twist knobs, and the bars took on a wider stance. The K3 style bar would last for three years ('72-'74) before it switched to a mirror mount lever perch. The bottom clamp was painted silver and the upper clamp that housed the twist knobs was solid aluminum.

The hand grips were redesigned. This time they had donut ends to keep the rider's hands on the bars and they were vented to give better airflow. The rear shocks on the 1972 K3 up to the 1974 K5 had a metal finished upper and lower cap that was lightly polished and clear coated.

The air cleaner was changed for '72 to a larger better flowing two-piece air breather. The air cleaner was held tightly in place by a frame mounted band secured with a 10mm bolt. This new design proved much better than the previous three years. It is very common to find hardtails with the air cleaner missing since they were just

1 year only smooth grain grid seat top with chrome side buttons

Chrome vented gas cap, K2-'78. Black tank decals on Candy Gold paint.

Rear fender without grommet plug and tire pressure decal-K3-K6.

Black plastic headlight bucket, K3-'78.

Welded bottom seam gas tank, used K3-K5.

pushed on and held by a small band clamp and screw.

Unlike the K2 with a rear foot pedal and dual hand brakes, the K3 eliminated the rear hand brake and went with a foot-operated brake pedal and front brake lever in aluminum with a black rubber tip. The K3 would set the tone for the way the Z50's would be set up for brakes and this was how the remaining bikes were built until the end of production in 1999.

All '72-'78 soft tails used the same style rear brake-rod set up. The complicated slide assembly that was used on the K2 was eliminated and replaced with a simple one-piece rod with a spring that mounted directly to the pedal. New for '72 on the shifter side of the frame was a clamp to hold the wire harness in place under the tank. The thick frame clamp would last until the end of the 1984 production year before it was changed to a wire version.

The gas tank was redesigned for the soft tail models. The tanks were more of a bubble style tank. The '72 K3 tank came with a large black graphic outlined in white with the word "Honda" in white and "Mini Trail" in orange outlined in white. This tank design would run from 1972-1978.

There are two versions of the gas tank that exist when looking to do a restoration. For the purists at heart not just any old '72-'78 tank will do. So don't just grab any tank that is sitting on the shelf in primer. The 1972 to 1974 (and based on the sales brochure possibly some of the early 1975 tanks) were crudely welded along the bottom seam whereas the majority of 1975-1978 tanks were stamped along the bottom seam of the tank.

By 1972, safety features were popping up on many products and the K3 was no different. The K3 was the first Mini Trail to have a bar mounted kill switch, a feature that was a sign of the times. The left side handlebar featured a headlight switch with the words on/off.

The taillight bracket, unlike those on the hardtail models, was mounted directly to the rear fender instead of on the fender and the frame like the K1 and K2 models. The taillight lens on all Z50A soft tails came without circle side reflectors made in the plastic, a feature that is only found on the K1 and K2 models. Just like the hardtails, the taillight lenses were made by Stanley. The foot peg assembly came in zinc plating and it had fold-up finned black rubber foot peg pads over black metal pegs.

The flywheel magneto covers for the first time featured the "Honda" logo highlighted in black paint; this paint filled logo cover design would carry on through the 1979 model year.

The headlight bucket was no longer metal; this time it was plastic with a chrome metal trim ring. This style bucket would stick around until the last Z50A rolled off the assembly line in 1978. The headlight bucket came with a black rubber gasket on the backside where the wires connected; this is a commonly missed part on a restoration and should not be overlooked.

The chrome gas cap was the K2 butterfly style and it would last until the end of the Z50A run in 1978. The tank warning decals were clear with black text on the candy gold model and on the light ruby red the text was silver. The top decal instructed the rider to read the owner's manual and the bottom decal warned the rider about wearing a helmet.

The parts books offer decals in white, black, and silver text for replacement purposes and they are not always true to the decals found on the bikes when they came from the factory. My advice is this; if you want to build your bike the way it came from the factory outfit it with the decal combinations I have given you.

All '72-'78 soft tails came with 37 tooth rear sprockets and a 76 link 420 chain. All soft tails used the redesigned compact gray TEC coil that mounted to the frame under the frame backbone below the seat.

The '72-'76 soft tails used a shorter throw chrome shifter than the hardtails. The kicker was changed from a bellowed out arm to a straight arm and remained in chrome until the end of the

The final chrome chain guard used in Z50 production. Note the clear vibration plug, a commonly missed part in restorations.

Polished and clear coated brake hubs and brake plates K3-K5.

K3 sales brochure.

Large round fold up foot pegs K3 & early K4.

K3 in Light Ruby Red.

K3 head tube tag.

1981 model year before switching to black. The brake hubs, plates, and cams were redesigned for '72. The rear hub this time came with mounting studs instead of a drilled hub with threads to accept bolts. It used a tongue washer and nuts to secure the rear sprocket. The '72-'74 brake hubs were polished aluminum with a clear coat. The hubs were redesigned for the soft tail models. They had notched out sections in them where the hub mounts up against the rim dish. The brake arms were enlarged for the soft tail models, most notably was the rear arm.

The wire harness and stators were changed for '72 and are interchangeable from '72-'75 models. No battery was used on the soft tail models.

The carburetor was changed for '72. They came with a rounded bottom bowl and a wider flat choke lever. The carburetor is interchangeable from '72-'75 and all feature a stamped "655 A" marking.

Like the cables and switches on the hardtails, the '72 K3 on up to the 1975 K6 used silver/gray casings. The stamped grade "8" hardware used on the Z50A soft tail models is the type that enthusiasts refer to as the pig-nose number 8.

No production numbers have been reported for the K3 model year. The Honda parts book references the rubber foot pegs to fit all bikes up to serial number 1019611. Phillip O'Guinn of Michigan owns an original light ruby red K3 with serial number 1019634 which is 23 higher than the Honda reference for rubber foot pegs. So once again this proves the parts books wrong and also helps firm up a general idea on the production numbers for this model year. At least 19,634 were produced.

Chapter 5

1973 Z50A K4

Engine beginning and ending serial numbers: 30000001 - 4999999
Frame beginning and ending serial numbers: 30000001 - Not Available
Carburetor serial number: 655 A

By November 1st of 1972, Honda had already released the second soft tail model, the 1973 K4. Oddly enough it was the third model produced in the same production year. The K2 finished up in April of 1972 and the K3 started production in January of 1972. K3 production ran until production started in November of 1972 for the K4.

For the most part the K4 was the same as the K3; however, it did undergo some changes and upgrades.

Like 1972, the '73 K4 came in two color options: Candy Orange and Hawaiian Blue Metallic. The tank band stripe on this model year was simple; it was black and white with a yellow Honda logo. The side cover decals were clear with silver text on the Hawaiian Blue model as well as the candy orange.

Just like the hardtail models, Honda liked to make changes mid-production on the soft tails and likewise did not mind using up parts until they were gone from previous models. The foot

Hawaiian Blue & Candy Orange K4 models.

All new for 1973 was a black chain guard. All upper chain guards would remain black through the end of production in 1999.

New aggressive black alligator style foot pegs. This concept would last until the end of production in 1999.

peg set up and the chrome chain guards were the parts Honda did away with mid production on the K4. Cameron Johnson owns a 1973 Z50A serial number 3004129 and a Candy Orange all original example that sports the early production K3 foot pegs/step bar and chrome chain guard.

New for the '73 K4 was the chain guard. It was switched to black and all future chain guards would come in black. Gone was the clear vibration plug, this time it was black and would remain black until the last Z50A rolled off the line in 1978.

The fold-up foot pegs had alligator teeth to keep the riders' feet on the pegs instead of rubber pads like the previous four years and like the K3 they came in black. To match the alligator foot pegs the step bar came in black instead of zinc and would remain black until the end of the Z50 production in 1999.

The tool kit plastic side cover matched the paint of the tank and fork and it came with a yellow "Z50" decal and a clear instructional decal with white text for transporting the Mini Trail. The seat was redesigned for '73. The box and grid pattern continued and would be used until the end of the '78 production, however new for '73 was a coarse grain top like the K2 model had. The back featured the stenciled "Honda" logo in silver.

The rear fender tire pressure decal said Z50A K4 in the top right corner. The decal was black with silver text. All other components remained the same for the K4, and just like the K3, production numbers are not available. Cameron Johnson owns a Hawaiian Blue K4 that is serial number 3013497. This particular K4 is the 13,497th off the line.

Transparent top of tank decals with white text.

2nd Generation pebble grain seat top. Rear tail light lens without side reflectors-K3-'78

An early "Cross Over" K4 model with left over large round K3 rubber pegs and chrome chain guard. Cameron Johnson Collection.

Cloud silver wheels, polished aluminum brake plates and hubs with a clear coat finish-K3-K5.

Chapter 6

1974 Z50A K5

Engine serial number beginning and ending: Z50AE-5000001 - 5999999
Frame number beginning and ending: Z50A 5000001 - 5033245
Carburetor serial number: 655 A

In 1974 the muscle car era was over. Gas prices were at an all-time high, Schwinn removed the stick shifts from the muscle bikes and this would be the last model year that Honda offered two color choices. It was a sign of the times. The 1974 K5 model could be purchased in either Candy Sapphire Blue or Candy Topaz Orange.

The tank stripe was yellow and black. The side cover came with a yellow and blue "Z" and a yellow "50" decal. Both the blue and orange bikes use silver text on the tank and side cover warning decals with the exception of the helmet warning decal which has white text.

The rear fender tire pressure decal said Z50A K5 in the top right corner. The decal is black with silver text.

Two rear fenders were used on the 1974 K5. The majority of K4s (30,721 of 33,245 produced) used the same fender that was used on the previous two model years. However, the rear fender underwent a subtle change most likely so it could be used on foreign market bikes. At serial

number 5030722 (30,722nd K4 produced) the rear fender had an oval shaped stamped hole in it and was plugged with a black rubber plug.

The 1973 Z50J required a larger style taillight bracket than the U.S. Z50A and thus used a rear fender with a hole to support the larger taillight bracket. Most likely as a way to cut costs and reduce the amount of parts that needed to be stocked in inventory. Honda introduced the 130 product code rear fender as a universal fender for both the foreign and domestic models.

The last 2,525 1974s, as well as the '75-'78, tire pressure decals dropped the "K" model identification in the top right corner and went with a universal "Z50A" identification in the top right corner.

Just like the rear fender, a few other parts on the K5 underwent some changes. The handle bars on the last 891 K5's changed over to the new style bar that would be used on all remaining Z50As. The new style bar had a mirror mount on the lever perch; otherwise it looked identical to the previous soft tail version.

The last 6,303 K5s used the redesigned throttle cable and the last 3,953 used the redesigned front brake cable. The K4-K5 seat design would be short lived and Honda would once again alter the seat for the K6 model. Just like with previous models, please keep in mind that

The last year Honda offered two color choices. Candy Topaz Orange and Candy Sapphire Blue were the color options for the Z50A K5.

Candy Topaz Orange tank & side cover with a black metal chain guard.

all of these serial number ranges/production figures for the parts changes should be used as a guide rather than as exact figures.

All other components remained the same as the previous model year.

Sales were very solid for 1974 and production reached 33,245 by sales end. Production would never hit these numbers again in the history of the Z50 Mini Trail.

Candy Sapphire Blue 1974 K5 Sales Brochure

Chapter 7
1975 Z50A K6

Engine serial number beginning and ending: Z50AE 6000001 - 6099999
Frame number beginning and ending: Z50A 6000001- -6005880
Carburetor serial number: 655 A

The 1975 K6 model was the last time Honda would refer to any of its Mini Trail 50s as a K Model.

The K6 came in Candy Ruby Red with an orange, yellow, and black decal on the tank. This was the first year that Honda went with one color option, a plan that would be the norm for the rest of the Z50 production. The top tank warning decals were clear with a silver/grayish text and were identical to the '72-'74 decals. This would be the last time Honda used this style decal configuration.

Cameron Johnson explains the side cover best. "The side cover featured a faded orange "Z" with a white "50" logo and the emblem was either printed directly onto the plastic or maybe was a water transfer decal that's cleared over, making it the only year that does not have an actual sticker." The transporting instructional decal on the side cover was clear with silver/grayish lettering to

Candy Ruby Red, the only color used in 1975-Contributor Huang Lam

Only side cover to have a water transfer decal versus a sticker.

This was the first year for painted hubs and brake plates as well as upper and lower shock tops.

match the tank warning decals.

1975 ushered in many new changes. At a glance one would not think so, however, many subtle things changed and it makes for a complicated restoration plan if you are not aware of the subtle differences. The early soft tails required the 120 product code part numbers and the K6-78 required the 130 product code part numbers.

New for 1975 was a rugged grain seat now with the Honda logo embossed into the rear of the seat back in standard black like the rest of the seat. No silver paint and stencils were used. The seat vinyl and foam were one piece molded and not sewn together like the previous models. The new seat design would carry on until the final Z50A was produced in 1978.

As mentioned earlier in the K5 section, the rear fender changed to the universal fender with the oval hole punched in it and plugged with a black rubber plug. This chrome style fender would be used until the end of the 1977 production year and the concept would carry over into the painted fender on the '78.

The front fender dropped the captured nuts on the mounting plate on the bottom of the fender like the previous three models had.

The handle bars also made a change to the 130 product code like the fenders and the seat. And like the last bars in the run for '74, all the '75-'78 bars had the mirror mount hole on the lever perch. New for 1975 were the front and rear hubs as well as brake plates in Silver paint. Gone were the polished aluminum parts, another sign of the times.

Just like the painted hubs, Honda switched to painted upper and lower shock tops to match the other aluminum components. The muffler stinger made a change, one that would carry on through the end of the 1978 production year. All other components remained the same as the previous soft tail model.

Production for this model was 5,880, certainly much lower than the previous year.

New for '75 an embossed Honda logo on the rear of the seat. Also new was the universal soft tail rear fender with the rubber plug.

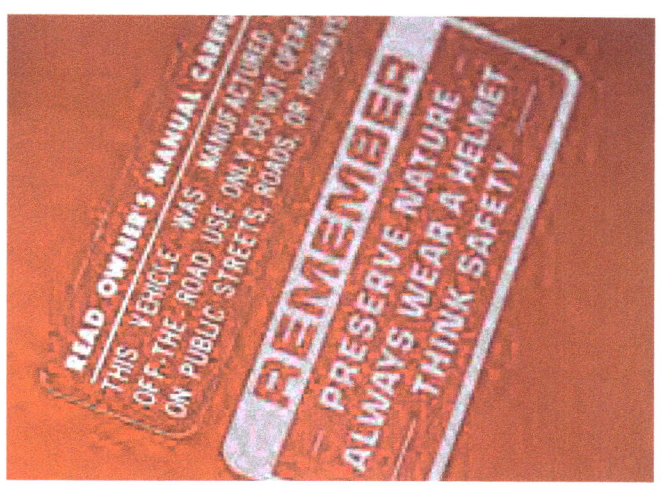

Candy Ruby Red tank with white warning decals.

First year for painted hubs and brake plates.

HONDA Z-50A K6

Candy Ruby Red 1975 K6 dealer brochure.

Circa 1975 K6 being enjoyed by a child.

Chapter 8

1976 Z50A

Engine serial number beginning and ending: Z50AE 6100001 - 6199999
Frame number beginning and ending: Z50A 6100001 - Not Available
Carburetor serial number: PA03A A

Because of the change in the Department of Motor Vehicle registration and title documentation process, for 1976 Honda started going by years, rather than K models, on all motorcycles.

The 1976 model came in Parakeet Yellow or as the sales brochure says, solid yellow with a bright red stripe on the side of the tank. The yellow side cover/tool kit cover on the shifter side has the words, "Z50" in red and white. The transporting decal switched from the long thin style decal to a more squared decal in clear with black text. The tank warning decals were also clear with black text.

The lower exhaust heat shield was switched

from chrome to flat black. The '76 would be the first Z50A to feature a black cased front brake cable and throttle cable. The left handlebar headlight switches along with the right side light switch underwent a change and came with black casings. New for '76 was a black triple clamp. This design would last until the end of the Z50A production in 1978.

The carburetor for '76 had a PA03A marking on it and this marking would be used on the '77 and 78' models as well. The stator and the wire harness made a product code change in 1976 and would remain the same through the end of the 1978 production year.

A unique feature that debuted on the '76 was the oil tube protector. It was a two-piece coil spring to protect the fuel line. It was also outfitted with a clamper bracket to secure the oil tube protector. This design would carry on for the remainder of the Z50A line.

For the first time Honda moved the tire pressure decal from the rear fender to the rear of the chain guard. This decal would remain on the chain guard until the end of Z50 production in 1999. The remaining components remained the same as the previous model year.

Production numbers are not known for the '76 Z50A model year. Cameron Johnson owns a 1976 with serial number 6105588 or the 5,588th 1976 produced.

New for 1976, an oil tube protector pictured on Cameron Johnson's all original Solid Yellow 1976 Z50A.

New large tank warning decal, new black kill switch wire casing, and new black triple clamp.

All new flat black lower exhaust heat shield.

First model to have a tire pressure decal on the chain guard.

New old stock solid yellow/parakeet yellow tool kit side Cover-Gary Lewis Collection.

First year for the black cased front brake cable and throttle cable.

One of Honda's early attempts at outreach to the female side of the market.

Chapter 9
1977 Z50A

Engine serial number beginning and ending: Z50AE 6200001 - 6299999
Frame number beginning and ending: Z50A 6200003 - 6219155
Carburetor serial number: PA03A A

The 1977 Z50A model came in Tahitian Red, a color that would span many model years. This was the first soft tail to feature the famous Honda wing, a symbol synonymous with Honda. The tank stripe was dark blue with a white pinstripe.

Gone were the days of rear buddy pegs and even if the soft tail models were not equipped with the mounting holes many people still rode double. For the '77 model year a decal was applied to the top front of the tank that read, "operators only no passengers".

The side cover paint matched the tank and it came with a yellow "Z" and white "50" decal with a black background. Below the Z50 decal was a clear transporting decal with black lettering.

Again most of the components resembled the previous soft tail model; however, this model used a slightly different foot brake pedal, the first of many to come in flat black. Like the '76, it featured a flat black lower heat shield and a

Tahitian Red 1977 Z50A-Ken Peare Collection

Z50AE 6114590, a left over 1976 engine on a 1977.

chrome upper shield.

To match the flat back lower heat shield, new for '77 was a flat black gear change shifter pedal. The black shifter design feature would stick around until the end of production in 1999. Production for this model was very solid once again with sales at 19,153 units.

Ken Peare of New Jersey owns one of the cleanest and certainly one of the most unique '77 Z50As around. Ken's '77 is serial number 6200145 making it the 143rd Z50A built. What is interesting about this bike is that the engine is serial number Z50AE-6114590 making it a late production 1976 engine. Another interesting thing about the Mini Trail is that it has a Bridgestone tire on the front and a Nitto tire on the rear. It is easy to see that by the condition of the motorcycle that the rims have the original blue factory markings and the engine bolts have never been cracked free from the frame. Both evidence that this is the way the motorcycle came from the factory. This is another great example of the oddities that one may encounter when dabbling in this hobby.

First year for the black gear shifter.

Chrome, rounded corner wide blade fuel cap, K2-'78. 3 piece transparent tank decals with black text on Tahitian Red paint.

First soft tail to feature a wing on the tank.

First Z50 to have a "rider only" decal on the tank.

First Z50 to feature a black foot brake pedal.

Nitto rear tire with a factory Bridgestone installed on the front.

Chapter 10

1978 Z50A

Engine serial number beginning and ending: Z50AE 6300001 - 9999999
Frame number beginning and ending: Z50A 6300003 - Not Available
Carburetor serial number: PA03A A

The 1978 Z50A would mark the last of the Z50A models. The '78 model once again came in Tahitian Red but this time with a yellow, orange, red, and black tank stripe sporting a gold Honda wing. The '78s came with a black frame, chain guard, front fork, plastic headlight bucket, taillight bracket, and rear shock coils. The '78 would be the last Mini Trail to have a metal chain guard. The chain guard came with a tire pressure decal in black with silver text. The foot brake pedal remained the same as the previous model year and came in black.

The '78 marked the first time in soft tail history that Honda went with painted steel fenders. The fenders were painted Tahitian Red to match the tank. The rear fender still came with the rubber plug like the '75-'77 models. Being that the painted fenders were only produced one year, trying to find a new old stock set today is very difficult as they are long discontinued and hard to come by. Collector and enthusiast Gary Lewis owns multiple sets of the N.O.S fenders, along with a match-

ing tank and side cover.

The orange tool kit side cover had a yellow with black outlined decal that said "Mini-Trail" and "50" in white that was also outlined in black. The '78 was the last Mini Trail to feature the verbiage on the right side engine oil/clutch cover.

The final Z50A seat came with the tough top grain material and the embossed rear Honda logo like the '75-'77 model years. This would be the last Mini Trail to feature the black rubber fork boots and the rounded corner butterfly on/off gas cap. The 1978 model was the last Mini Trail to feature a separate bar mounted on/off kill switch assembly.

Production numbers are not available for this year.

1978 owned by Cameron Johnson. The only soft tail with painted steel fenders.

Last model to use a metal chain guard.

Final model to use the chrome vented butterfly gas cap K3- '78.

Chapter 11
1979 Z50R

Engine serial number beginning and ending: AB02E 5000001-5099999
Frame number beginning and ending: AB02 5000009 - AB02 5024801
Carburetor serial number: PA03B A

For the 1979 model year, Honda revamped the Mini Trail and the model name. Instead of another Z50A, a model name that had been in production since 1968, the new model name was changed to Z50R. It was a sign of the times, and racing dirt bike style motorcycles were the in-thing and Honda was at it again with the all new Z50R.

They did away with the majority of chrome parts and the headlights and taillights. They traded that design for low gloss black painted components and lots of plastic.

The headlight was replaced by a plastic front number plate and a side number plate to match. The lone side number plate had a red and black "Z" logo with a white "50R" logo below it. The front and rear fenders and number plates were solid plastic and Tahitian Red in color.

The muffler and foot pedal were low gloss black. The rear shocks were also black with silver

painted upper and lower covers; a design scheme that would carry on until the last 1983 rolled off the line.

The '79 has a really skinny stem on the kickstand. It along with the foot peg assembly is also low gloss black.

The easy transport fold-down handlebars were also a thing of the past and were replaced by high-rise Motocross style handlebars. The first Z50R model is often times referred to as the "high bar" model; sort of like the first Z50A model. It is the only Z50R model with this style handlebar.

The year 1979 was the first Mini Trail to incorporate the on/off kill switch and the hand brake lever all in one unit. The on/off assembly came in aluminum with a matching black tipped aluminum brake lever. It is also the only Z50R model without some sort of side art logo on the seat. The seat came in a rugged grain and had a white Honda logo on the back.

This model also featured a very unique muffler and upper muffler guard heat shield. The muffler heat shield is very large and unique because it does not have a cut out for a number plate bracket and plate. This was the only model to feature this type of exhaust system.

Only Z50R to feature high rise handlebars.

First model to use plastic number plates.

The '79 came in Tahitian Red with a gold Honda logo on the tank; a tank design that would last until the end of the 1984 line. The '79 model was also the last model to sport the round hole rim dishes like the Z50A's had.

This would be the first Mini Trail to feature a black plastic air box, a style that would be used until the last '99 model rolled off the assembly line. Keeping with the plastic parts, the '79 also featured a short style chain guard similar to the length of the '72-'78 style, but this time in black plastic. The unique thing about the chain guard sticker on this model is that Honda used up left over tire pressure decals from the previous model year. This is evident because the decal on early as well as late production '79s say Z50A on them instead of Z50R. The throttle cable on this model is very unique. It is the only one that does not have a curved bend in the metal sleeve that screws into the on/off switch/throttle assembly.

All new plastic chain guard. It features the left over Z50A stickers from the previous year & not a Z50R sticker.)

New for '79 was a flat chrome gas cap with the word "gas" engraved in the top with no on/off butterfly. No breather tube was used on this model. This style gas cap would be used until the end of the '82 model year. This was the first Mini Trail to not have verbiage on the clutch/oil cover. This design would last until the end of 1999. The 1979 Mini would be the last Mini Trail to feature the black text in the center of the points cover on the flywheel cover. Aside from the '86 Z50RD, the '79 was the last Mini Trail to feature a chrome kick starter arm.

The redesigned Mini Trail was a huge success. By the end of production, Honda sold 24,793 Mini Trails.

Last model to use the round hole Z50A style rims.

Chapter 12

1980 Z50R

Engine serial number beginning and ending: AB02 5100001 - 5199999
Frame number beginning and ending: AB02 5100007 - 5110396

The 1980 model year saw many noticeable changes, changes that would set the tone for many years to come. An exception would be the Tahitian Red color scheme, which remained the same as the previous year as did the tank graphics.

The high rise handlebars were a thing of the past and a newly designed black low style Motocross bar with black rubber grips, aluminum on/off kill switch with matching rubber tipped aluminum lever was mounted on a black triple clamp. This style bar and grip would last until the end of production in 1999.

The complete exhaust system was changed again. The upper exhaust heat shield was much smaller than the previous model and featured three vent holes. This time the new design would last until the end of the '87 model year. The seat had a red "Z" logo on each side and a traditional Honda logo on the rear in white. The side logo design scheme on seats was new for 1980 and would last until 1999.

Instead of one side number plate and one on the front, the '80 model had a Tahitian Red number plate on each side with a large white "50R" decal as well as a Tahitian Red plate on the front. The three

number plate design would carry on through the '87 production.

The '80 model was the first Mini Trail to have the large kidney bean slotted holes in the rim dishes and just like the previous years they were cloud silver. The new rims had a three-bolt hole mounting set up, instead of four to hold the redesigned matching cloud silver

Top: First year for a side seat logo and the metal lower chain guard. Red "Z" seat logo and a large White "50R" number plate decal and Tahitian Red lower metal chain guard.

Middle: Keeping with tradition, the rear of the seat featured the "Honda" logo in white.

Bottom: Zinc coated kick starter arm- 1980-1981. A new rugged foot brake pedal and newly designed exhaust heat shield configuration that would last until the end of production in 1987.

Z50R. AN EXCITING FIRST FROM HONDA.

Your first motorcycle.
You talked to your friends. Read all the literature. And got the OK from the folks. Now it's time to choose.
Fortunately, Honda's got an easy answer. The Z50R. Because Honda knows better than anyone what a first-ever motorcycle is all about.
For starters, the Z50R is a Honda four-stroke. Quiet and predictable. And that 49 cc OHC single is one of the toughest engines Honda has ever made. Proven on literally hundreds of thousands of motorcycles around the world. Some call it the bullet proof mini.
Easy to ride? You bet. An automatic clutch takes the fuss out of shifting gears. But not the fun. Because the wide-ratio three-speed transmission shifts quick and easy. And the seat height is only 23 inches, so up-and-comers don't have to stretch to reach the ground. And at 109.1 pounds dry, there's not a lot of weight to wrestle with. Nice and easy.
The Z50R is a mini. But not a mouse. It's loaded with lots of the same trick features found on Honda's full-size off-road blasters. Block pattern tires. Front and rear drum brakes. Heat-shielded exhaust with USDA-approved spark arrestor. And with a competition style seat and number plate, it's red hot, rugged and ready.
The Z50R. This tricked-out, easy-riding Honda is right. From the start.

HONDA FOLLOW THE LEADER.

BILL BROWNELL
HONDA TRIUMPH
231 NORD AVENUE
CHICO, CALIF. 95926

49 cc four-stroke single is world famous for reliability.

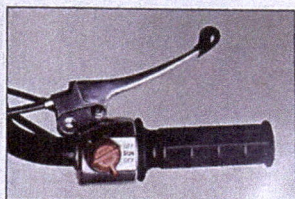
Brake and throttle levers are scaled down to fit an up-and-comer's grip.

Folding steel footpegs are cleated for sure footing.

The Z50R is outfitted with a competition number plate, just like Honda's full-size motocross racers.

1980 Z50R SPECIFICATIONS

Engine .... 49 cc OHC four-stroke single	Width .... 23.8 inches
Starter .... Kick	Height .... 31.9 inches
Clutch .... Automatic	Seat Height .... 22.6 inches
Transmission .... Three-speed	Tires .... 3.50-8 block pattern
Length .... 51.2 inches	Dry Weight .... 109.1 pounds
	Color .... Red

ALWAYS WEAR A HELMET AND EYE PROTECTION. Designed for off-road, operator use only. Specifications and availability subject to change without notice. © 1979 American Honda Motor Co., Inc. Printed in U.S.A.   A0062

painted front and rear hubs. This setup would carry on throughout the rest of the Mini Trail line up.

The chain guard was extended this time and the new chain guard would last until the end of production in '99. This model was also the first to feature a lower metal chain guard and like the other components it was Tahitian Red to match the frame. Like the longer chain guard, the lower metal chain guard would last until the end of production in 1999. The tire pressure decal in silver with black text was placed on the chain guard.

The foot brake pedal was redesigned for 1980, this time it was a thin metal bar similar to the thickness of the K2 pedal. The diamond pattern footpad was replaced with a cut out smaller version with rugged teeth around the edges. The pedal came in black and would remain black until the end of production in 1999.

The kick starter was changed from a chrome style to a zinc finished version. This design would only last two years before undergoing another change. The rear brake rod was changed to a simpler one-piece version with a slight bend in the end instead of the knuckle joint two-piece unit that the '77-'79 models used. The rear shocks had silver painted upper and lower covers and black shock coil springs.

The flywheel covers reverted back to the look of the hardtails and went with no black paint in the Honda logo on the points cover. This no-paint-in-text look would carry on through the end of the '87 model year before the cover was changed again.

In all, 10,390 Mini Trails were sold in 1980, less than half of what was sold the previous year.

Chapter 13
1981 Z50R

Engine serial number beginning and ending: AB02E-5200001 - AB02E-5299999
Frame number beginning and ending: JH2AB020*BS200002 - JH2AB020*BS211751
Carburetor serial number: PA03C A

The 1981 model year was almost identical to the previous model. The only difference between the 1980 and 1981 was the decal on the side number plates. The "50" was in white and the "R" was in red. The 1981 model was the final Z50 with a zinc metal finish kick-starter arm.

Production numbers aside, Gregg Davidian knows the difficulty level of trying to acquire a low hour survivor 1980-82 Z50R, "They're just not out there, and new old stock seats for the early '80s models don't exist."

"When Gary Lewis of Michigan delivered one of the lowest hour 1981 Z50Rs to me several years ago reality set in at how low the production number is on the early '80s models. The number plate decals are usually always torn or missing." Certainly a big deal when as stated earlier it is one of the main differences that separates '80 from '81.

11,750 Mini Trails were sold in 1981, slightly up from the previous year.

Number plate sticker "50" in white and "R" in red.

Front of 1981 Dealer Sales Brochure

Back of 1981 sales Brochure.

Back of the Honda Junior Rider Brochure.

Front of the Honda Junior Rider Brochure.

Black Upper plastic chain guard with Tahitian Red metal lower chain guard. 1980-1982.

Chapter 14
1982 Z50R

Engine serial number beginning and ending: AB02E-5300001 - AB02E-5399999
Frame number beginning and ending: JH2AB020*CS300002 - JH2AB020*CS317543
Carburetor serial number: PA03D A

The 1982 model saw some noticeable style changes. The first being the color. Instead of being Tahitian Red it came in Blaze Red. The Blaze Red color scheme actually resembled more of an orange color than red, and it would be used for many years.

The seat-side graphics were changed to a white "50R" logo with a white Honda logo on the back of the seat. The side number plates were Ceramic White and had a red "Z" logo on them. Fenders, both front and rear, matched the frame and tank and were also Blaze Red. The top head cover

featured a new design look, one that would carry on until the end of production in 1999. The new design featured a vertical and horizontal pattern to help cool the head. The previous models had a vertically finned pattern.

1982 was the first model to come with a black oxide kick start arm to match the foot pedal, pegs, and shifter. The black painted components would continue to the end of the 1999 production.

Another new feature for '82 was the use of engine fasteners, instead of case screws. Honda switched to a flange head screw so you could use a box end or open end wrench as well as a nut driver to add or remove the hardware. This eliminated the chance of rounding out the heads and made for easier maintenance.

By year's end, 17,542 Mini Trails were produced.

White "50R" seat logo with Ceramic White number plates with a red "Z".

Upper exhaust heat shield 1980-1987. Lower heat shields used 1980-1999.

First year for Blaze Red paint.

First year for the black kick starter arm.

Chapter 15
1983 Z50R

Engine serial number beginning and ending: AB02E-5400001 - AB02E-5499999
Frame number beginning and ending: JH2AB020*DS400012 - JH2AB020*DS408789
Carburetor serial number: PA03D A

The 1983 model would be the last Mini Trail to have a black seat. The seat had a white "Z" logo on each side and the traditional Honda script on the back. This time the number plates were bright yellow and they sported white "Z50R" graphics. Just like the previous model year, the '83 was finished in Blaze Red paint and matching plastic fenders.

New for '83 was a chrome, vented gas cap with a black breather tube that rested in the center of the chrome steering stem nut. The lower chain guard was switched from Blaze Red to black for '83. All other components remained the same as the previous year.

Sales totaled 8,778 Mini Trails by years' end.

Chapter 16

1984 Z50R

Engine serial number beginning and ending: AB02E-5500001 - AB02E-5599999
Frame number beginning and ending: JH2AB020*ES500001 - JH2AB020*ES517905
Carburetor serial number: PA03D A

The 1984 model continued the tradition of the previous two years with the Blaze Red painted and plastic parts, as well as the bright yellow number plates. This time the number plates had red "50R" graphics outlined in black to match the new rear shock coils.

This would be the last model year to carry the traditional gold Honda wing with the "Honda" script below it. For the first time in Mini Trail history Honda went with a blue seat. The seat was enhanced with a white "Z" logo on each side and a white Honda logo on the back. All other components remained the same as the previous model year.

Production topped out at 17,905 and a new design scheme was just around the corner.

First blue seat and Bright Yellow number plates with Red "50R" decals.

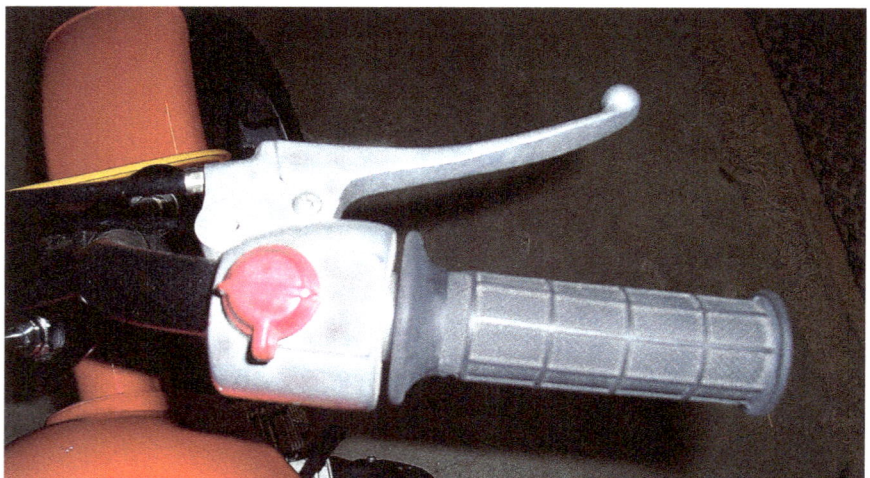

Left: Black grips with an aluminum front brake lever and on/off kill switch.

Left: Blaze Red rear shock coils.

Chapter 17

1985 Z50R

Engine serial number beginning and ending: AB02E-5600001 - AB02E-5699999
Frame number beginning and ending: JH2AB020*FS600001 - Not Available
Carburetor serial number: PA03D A

The 1985 model came with Blaze Red paint and matching plastic fenders, while number plates remained bright yellow - and this was the final time that this color would be used. This was the first year that the number plates did not feature any graphics.

The rear shocks were painted silver on top and bottom and had blue coils to match the seat. The seat featured a "Z" in white with a matching white Honda logo on the back of the seat. The tank was Blaze Red and the decal was a brand new design. This time it featured a red, white, and blue Honda wing with "50R" below the wing. The "50R" was white on the top and blue on the bottom.

New for 1985 was a frame mounted thin-wire cable and harness holder that stuck outside of the frame under the tank. This new design would last until the end of Mini Trail production in 1999. IRC Tractor Grip tires came mounted on silver

slotted wheels, hubs, and brake plates. 1985 was the last year of the aluminum tipped lever with the black rubber knob on the end. All other components remained the same as the previous model year.

Production numbers are not available for this model year.

Blaze Red Paint and plastic fenders

Bright Blue seat with large White "Z" logo.

Yellow number plates & first year without number plate decals

First year for the frame mounted thin-wire cable and harness holder

New Red, White, & Blue Honda wing tank decal.

Last year of the aluminum lever with the black rubber tips.

All new blue rear shocks.

Cloud Silver slotted wheels, hubs and brake plates 1980-1985.

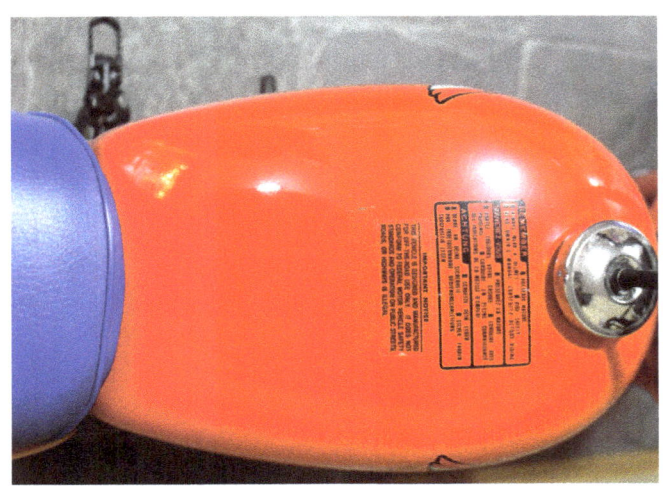

Chrome vented gas cap with breather tube, 1983-1987

Back side of original sales brochure-Jason Bruce collection

Chapter 18

1986 Z50R

Engine serial number beginning and ending: AB02E-5700001 - AB02E-5799999
Frame number beginning and ending: JH2AB020*GS700001 - GS711651
Carburetor serial number: PA03F A

For the 1986 model year, Honda had a "Special" surprise up their sleeve. For 1986 you could purchase a Z50R or you could purchase a Z50RD.

The Z50R was the first Mini Trail to have gold wheels, a feature that would prove to be highly desirable for collectors in years to come. The new gold wheels, hubs, and brake plates came mounted on IRC Tractor Grip tires or Bridgestone Trail Wing 2 tires. The rear shocks were painted gold on top and bottom to match the wheels and had blue coils to match the seat.

The seat was blue again this year; however, this time it featured a large white "Z" logo and a white Honda logo on the back. Gone were the yellow number plates, this time Honda went with three Shasta White number plates, again with no graphics. The tank color once again was

Blaze Red. The graphics on the tank were similar to those on the '85 model, however the "50" was white and the "R" was blue. The gas cap was chrome with a black rubber venting tube that mounted in the hole of the steering stem center nut. Like the frame and tank, the plastic fenders were Blaze Red to match.

The handle bars were BMX style and they came in semi-gloss black with black Hand grips. A non-rubber tipped aluminum brake lever mounted in the aluminum on/off switch assembly was mounted on the right side of the bar like previous model years with this feature. The rest of the components remained the same as the previous model year.

Collectors tend to prefer the Z50RD over the '86 Z50R, but that wasn't always the case. Gregg Davidian remembers working for Honda in the 1980's and recalls the interest in the Z50 models. "When the '86 came out nobody wanted the Christmas Special, everyone went for the orange and blue R and the RDs just sat on the floor". For many years the RD didn't bring the attention on the internet, but that has changed over the past 5 years.

The reality is, for every 10 or maybe 20 Z50RDs that come up for sale you might find one '86 Z50R. To find a clean original '86 Z50R continues to be a challenge. The Z50RD's as a whole were taken better care of than the Z50Rs, which is why it is so difficult to find a clean, Z50R survivor.

I have always said in the toy collecting world that if the package says "limited edition" then chances are they made millions of them. Whether or not the words "Special" appear on top of an '86 tank, both versions are highly collectible and like all Mini Trails, clean survivors are becoming more and more difficult to find.

Production Numbers for the Z50R and RD combined totaled 11,651 units.

What could be better than a Dad who bought you a new Honda Mini Trail?

Gold wheels, 1986-1987 Z50R.

Blue seat-1986-1987, blue rear shocks- 1986-1987, Shasta White number plates- 1986-1987, & Blaze Red paint and fenders.

Chapter 19

1986 Z50RD

Engine serial number beginning and ending: AB02E-5700001 - AB02E-5799999
Frame number beginning and ending Z50RD: JH2AB020*GS700001 - GS710561

The Z50RD was a "Special Edition" model produced exclusively for the 1986 year. Production started around late July/early August of 1985.

The "D" letter that was added to the "R" model stood for "dealer." The RDs came two to a crate. The advertising ploy on the RD was that it was supposed to be a Christmas "Special", the top tank decal even said special. Honda tried to market the Mini Trail with Christmas ornaments that dealers were given to hang around the dealerships. Jason Bruce of Florida owns an original set of Christmas ornaments and proudly displays them with his Mini Trail collection.

The most commonly asked question on the RDs is, how many were made? A few stories exist as to how many were allocated and how many were actually produced. Some enthusiasts say that only the top selling Honda dealers were eligible to receive them while others claim that every dealer

was given two (one crate).

The exact production numbers are uncertain because the 1986 production figures include both the Z50R and the RD. A total of 11,651 Mini Trails were produced in 1986. J.C. Davidson of Racine, Wisconsin owns the 498th Z50RD made, and it was built in August of 1985. District sales manager for Polaris, Ryan Hoffman of Edmonton Alberta, Canada, owns both a Z50RD and a Z50R. The RD is the 2,702nd '86 model made and his Z50R is the 11,282nd '86 produced. So as you can see by these examples the Rs and RDs are mixed throughout the production with one exception. The last RD produced was serial number 710561 and the serial number for the last R was 711651. Wintery weather in many regions of the country and Christmas having passed could have played a significant role in the final production run - being that just Z50R's were produced in the final months.

Many Mini Trail enthusiasts believe that between 2,500-3,000 RD models were produced. An interesting fact about the production number is that if each dealer truly only received two RD's then the production numbers should be much lower because as of the late 1980's there were only 805 Honda dealers.

Long time Mini Trail collector Gregg Davidian

1986 Z50RD Christmas Special

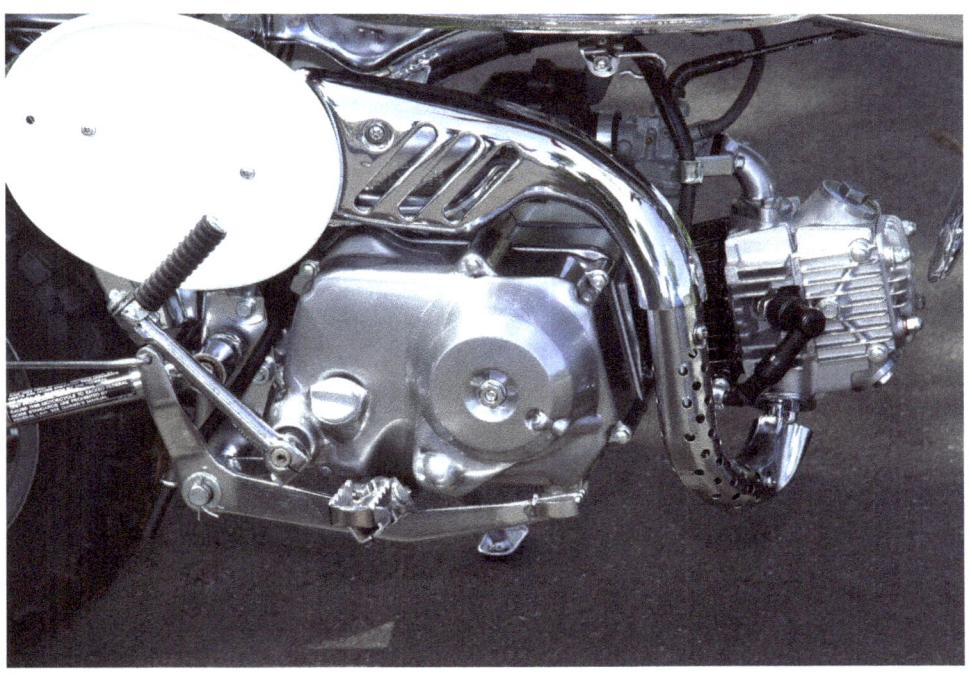

Polished aluminum clear coated engine case covers with fully chromed exhaust system.

of New Jersey worked at a Honda dealership in the 1980s. When asked about the Z50RD he exclaimed, "They were a tough sell, everyone wanted to buy the Z50R, you couldn't give the RD away, and many RDs sat and took a while to sell." Lately the Z50RD has gained "Cult Status" and many collectors refer to them as "Chromies".

Nice complete bikes, restored examples, and new old stock parts have fetched a pretty penny lately for this "Special" one-year model. Gregg currently owns a crate with two original RDs still strapped in from the day they left Japan. The serial numbers on these two bikes are not consecutive. Certainly a unique item and a rare find.

Shasta White plastic number plates, chrome wheels with polished aluminum & clear-coated brake hubs and brake plates.

What exactly makes an RD so "special"? The RD featured an all chrome look. All metal parts were chromed. All RD models came outfitted with red rubber hand grips and a red seat with a large outlined white "Z" logo and white Honda logo on the back. It is the same design as the '86 Z50R blue version.

Some interesting bits of information to keep in mind when restoring an RD or looking to purchase one is that on the original RDs the left side grip has a water release hole in the end of it and the throttle grip does not. The N.O.S. grips are smooth on both ends and the reproduction grips have water release

Chrome rear shocks & red seat with Shasta White outlined "Z" side graphics.

holes in both grips.

Just like the '86 Z50R, the RD came with white number plates with no graphics. The clutch cover and flywheel cover were lightly polished and clear coated; a unique feature to this model Mini Trail.

An all chrome muffler exhaust system set it apart from all soft tails, it is the only model other than the hardtails to feature this type of exhaust system. The RD is also the only Mini Trail to feature chrome rims and matching chrome wheel hardware. The hubs and brake plates were done in the same finish to match the covers.

The tank warning decals were identical to the '86 R with the addition of the "Special" decal above the warning decals. If you were to purchase a replacement tank from Honda, the "Special" decal was the only one that came on the tank. These tanks have long been discontinued and today can fetch upwards of $1,000 or more in N.O.S. condition.

The chain guard came in black plastic like the "R" version. The decal was a brushed aluminum finish and was stuck to the black plastic. The swing arm also had an exhaust warning decal just like the Z50R with the production date on it.

Simply put, the red parts and the chrome look are what set it apart, the remaining components remained the same as the '86 Z50R. As mentioned above, my friend Gregg Davidian owns a pair of 1986 Z50RDs still in the crate. They were originally purchased March 16th 1989 from Snyder's Honda of Manhattan, Kansas. They changed hands several times before Gregg acquired them about 15 years ago. I spoke with the owner of the now defunct dealership and he said he knows he sold 3, but possibly 4 crates worth of RDs. He said he was a "D" level dealership, the lowest level dealership and believes Honda produced more like 5,000 to 6,000 based on the allotment he was given.

The burning question in anyone's mind when they hear about or see a motorcycle still in the crate is, why? When I asked Mr. Snyder about the Z50RD's in the crate he said he had a plan

Black plastic upper chain guard with brushed aluminum tire pressure decal and a chrome lower chain guard.

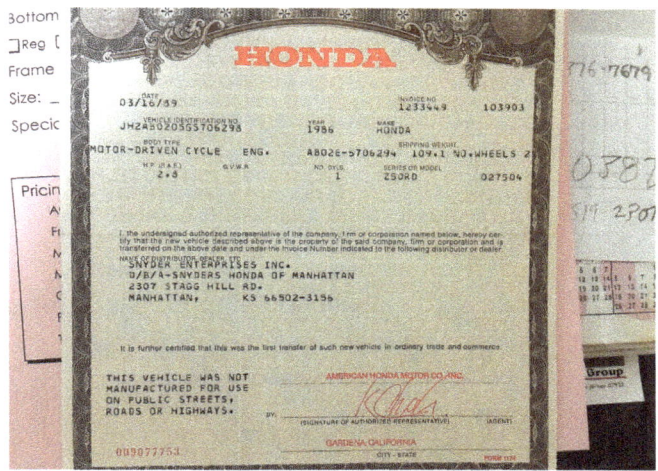
An original Honda Manufactures statement of origin for an '86 Z50RD

Red hand grips, aluminum non rubber tipped black lever, on/off kill switch, and chrome handle bar.

Christmas Specials still in the crate, originally sold March 16th 1989 by Snyder's Honda in Manhattan Kansas-Gregg Davidian collection.

Christmas Specials with serial numbers 6,154 & 6,298.

to keep them for twenty years and then sell them off. A likely story, but after holding onto them for just over three years he found that he needed money for his son's college tuition so the first thing he could think to sell was the RDs. He sold them through the Snyder Honda dealership so the titles show the dealer name and most interestingly as mentioned before they are dated March 16th 1989. You might be wondering how much he got for the pair 3 years after they were built. He sold them for $5,000.00 in the crate. A hefty price considering they were only 3 years old and only a speculation of what was yet to come.

The Z50RD model turned 30 years old as of 2016. How amazing would it be to own a brand new set still in the factory Honda crate with all of the original paperwork? Gregg Davidian can't keep track of the number of times that people claimed they had a pair of RD's still in the crate or other years for that matter. "It is always the same song and dance. No pictures ever transpire or people use my pictures and the people vanish when you try to pursue them." If you are interested in owning the only set known to exist, they are for sale and I can assist the buyer in purchasing them from Gregg.

The serial numbers of Gregg's two Mini Trails are 144 apart. Out of 11,651 total 1986 Z50Rs and RDs produced, these particular RD's are the 6,154th and 6,298th produced. How many RD's were made? Documentation is limited so it remains a mystery as to how many were manufactured.

Original 1986 dealer display Christmas "Special" Ornaments -Jason Bruce collection.

Chapter 20
1987 Z50R

Engine serial number beginning and ending: AB02E-5800001 - AB02E-5899999
Frame number beginning and ending Z50RD: JH2AB020*HS800001 - HS803002
Carburetor serial number: PA03F A

The 1987 Honda Z50R resembled the '86 model in many ways. The fuel tank once again came in Blaze Red and had the same tank decals. It also had the same blue seat with the large white outlined "Z" logo and Honda name on the back as the 1986 Z50R. It would be one of just two models to feature the coveted gold wheels.

This would be the first time Honda used a Shasta White frame, fenders, and rear shocks to showcase their new Mini trail. The rear shocks had white coils and silver painted tops and bottoms. A black, plastic chain guard and a semi-gloss black lower chain guard protected the rider.

Blaze Red number plates were used on the final bubble tank model. Nine years had passed and the '87 model was the last of the "fat tank" or "bubble tank" Mini Trails. Production on the '87 model was remarkably low compared to the previous model year. Ryan Hoffman of Canada owns the original example seen here, one of the

117

few remaining quality examples of the low production '87 Z50R. New old stock tanks and seats can fetch high prices, and parts are getting harder and harder to come by. In all, 3,002 units were sold and this was the beginning of a downward trend in Mini Trail sales.

Above: The final Z50R with the signature tear drop fat style tank

Below: 1986-1987 Blaze Red tank with a Red, White, & Blue decal. Unlike 1985, "50" came in White and "R" in Blue.

Shasta White frame & plastic fenders.

Gold wheels, 1986-1987.

Blaze Red number plates.

Red, White, & Blue tank decal 1986-1987 & final year for the chrome vented gas cap.

Final 3-speed transmission with a down shift pattern.

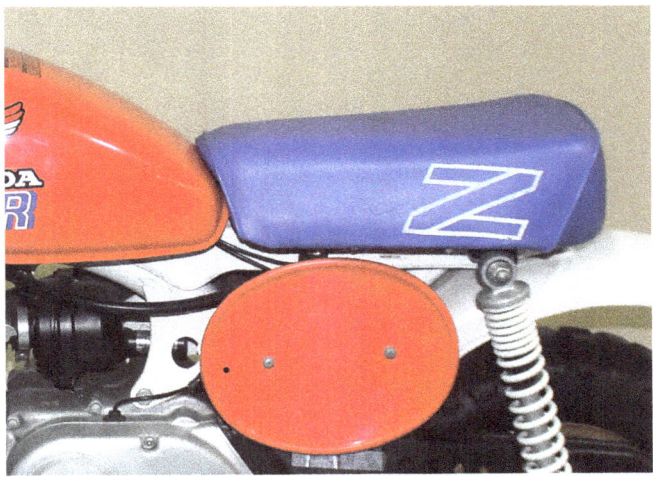
Bright Blue seat with large stenciled "Z" side logo-1986-1987. Final year for the close gap rear shock coils.

Chapter 21

1988 Z50R

Engine serial number beginning and ending: AB02E-5900001 - AB02E-5999999
Frame number beginning and ending Z50RD: JH2AB020*JS900005 - JS903187
Carburetor serial number: PA03H A

The 1988 Z50R model for the first time ever featured a C.D.I. or capacitor discharge ignition system. The '88 model was the 20th anniversary edition and it had a sticker price of $798.00.

New for '88 was a redesigned tank. The tank is a flat-back design to allow the new dirt bike slope-style seat to lock into it. It came in Blaze Red with a large white "Z" logo outlined in gray with a small "50R" all in white.

This model featured the redesigned blue seat with the Honda logo in bold white lettering on both sides as well as the rear of the seat. The frame, front fork, rear swing arm, wheels, front fender, and rear shocks also sported the Shasta White color scheme.

All new for 1988 was a large square front number plate in Shasta White. To enhance the look, the number plate featured a red vinyl decal

with the word Honda in stencil white block lettering. This would be the only Mini Trail to feature a front number plate decal.

The rear shocks were redesigned and had a wider spacing pattern than the previous years. The front fender was redesigned and was wider and shorter in stature than the previous model years.

For the first time in Mini Trail history, Honda used a rear tail assembly in place of a single rear fender. The rear tail came in Blaze red with Shasta White vinyl number plates. The exhaust system was completely changed from the muffler to the upper and lower heat shields and it really muffled the sound.

The engine oil cover as well as the flywheel cover were changed up and came in a gold metal tone finish. To match the black handle bars, new-for-'88 was a black on/off kill switch fitted with a black metal hand brake lever.

By the end of the Z50R production run, 3,183 1988 Z50Rs were produced. This was only 181 more than the previous year; however, consumers had an on-road choice in the ZB50, and that may have had a little to do with the sales figures.

Final Blue seat used in the Z50 line. Bike stand from PhatMX Motorcycle Parts Supply-courtesy of owner Keith Walker

Above: The only Z50 to feature a front number plate decal.

Left: Black bars & black on/off switch 1988-1989. New shock design for 1988 with fewer coils used until end of production in 1999.

Chapter 22
1989 Z50R

Engine serial number beginning and ending: AB02E-6000001 - AB02E-6099999
Frame number beginning and ending: JH2AB020*KS000001 - JH2AB020*KS002752
Carburetor serial number: PA03H B

The 1989 Mini Trail was almost the last Mini Trail produced for the U.S. market. Prices were rising on the Mini Trail and there were plenty of other things kids were interested in that may have played a part in the declining sales. The BMX market was in its prime, Nintendo was pumping out new games left and right, and the baseball card world had seen more new brands pop up than ever before.

The '89 model featured an all red rear tail with Shasta White vinyl number plate side graphics.

The front fender, seat, and tank all came in red. The seat featured an all-white "Z" on each side. The tank featured a new wing design in all white and it said "50R" below it in white, and outlined in gray.

The oil clutch cover and the flywheel cover were a gold tone metal flake like the previous year. Likewise, the rear shocks, wheels, frame, triple clamp, front fork, and rear swing arm were painted Shasta White - just like the previous year.

New for '89 was a set of Shasta White handlebars to match the majority of the Mini Trail's painted

components. The Shasta White handlebar paint scheme would remain the norm for the remainder of the Mini Trail run. The year 1989 would be the final time Honda used a black on/off kill switch on a Mini Trail.

The front number plate did not feature any vinyl decals or Honda logos like the previous model. It was simply just a Shasta White plastic number plate. The exhaust, along with the other components remained basically the same as the previous model year.

Jason Bruce of Florida and Ryan Hoffman of Canada own two of the cleanest original examples of '89 Z50Rs that I've seen. Like most Mini Trails it is difficult to find one that has been well preserved with an un-dented tank and un-ripped seat. Jason has the title, warranty card, and original bill of sale. Jason's '89 was purchased on June 30th of 1990 in Greensboro North Carolina. It is the 350th '89 made out of the 2,752 produced.

The price on the 1989 Z50R might have been an indication as to why sales were at an all-time low. $1,220.00 for a mini bike in the 1980's certainly was not in most people's budget. No matter what the reason for the low production and sales numbers, the slow sales of the 1989 models did affect Honda's plans for the 1990 model. In the end they decided to skip the year entirely. You can't buy a 1990 Z50R because Honda didn't build a Mini Trail in 1990.

Black on/off kill switch and gold tone flywheel cover and clutch cover, both 1988-1989 exclusive components.

Shasta White and Gray "50R" tank decal with a Shasta White Honda wing. Red tank, tail, seat, and front fender.

123

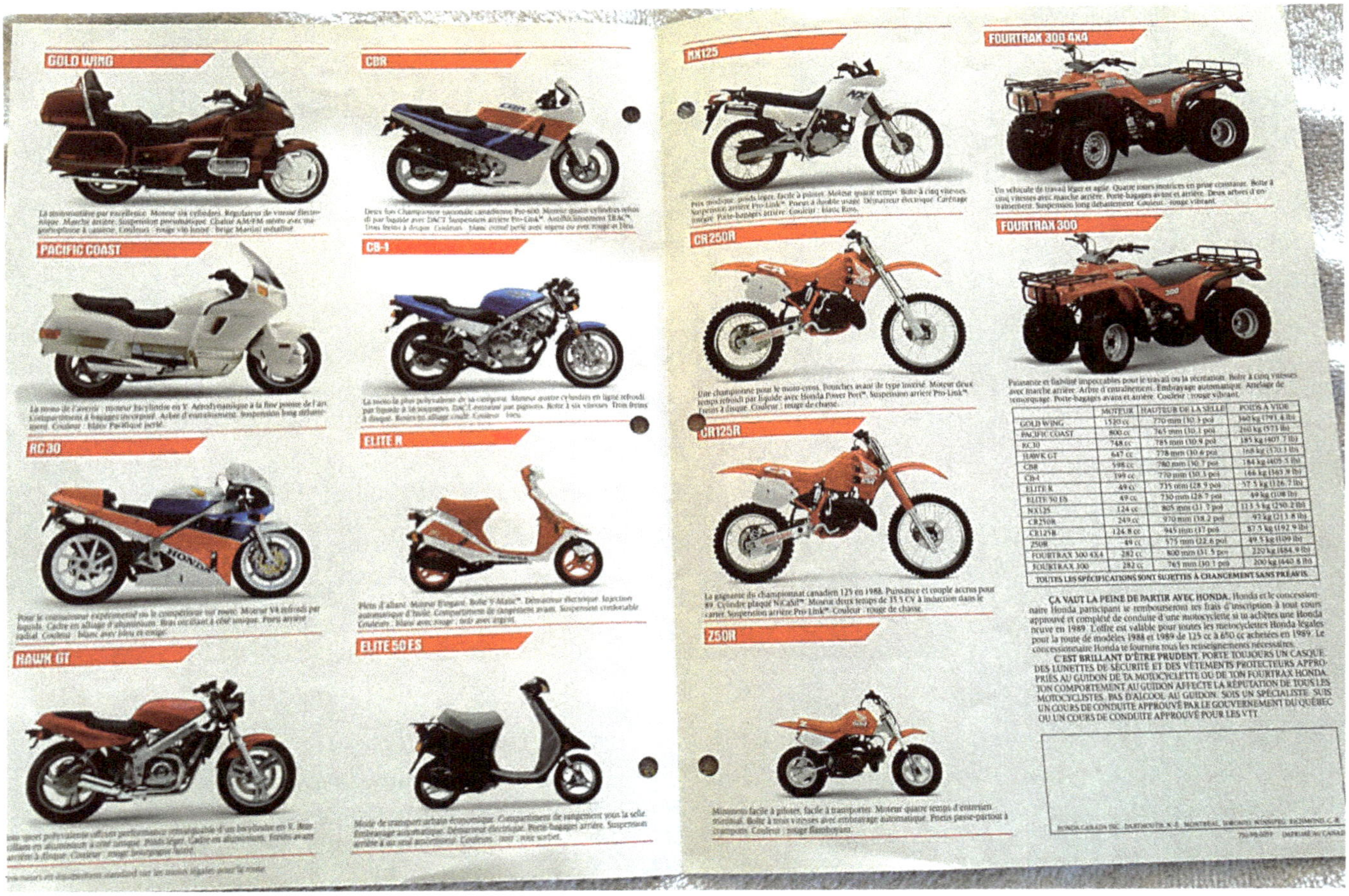

GOLD WING
CBR
NX125
FOURTRAX 300 4X4
PACIFIC COAST
CB-1
CR250R
FOURTRAX 300
RC30
ELITE R
CR125R
HAWK GT
ELITE 50 ES
Z50R

	MOTEUR	HAUTEUR DE LA SELLE	POIDS À VIDE
GOLD WING	1520 cc	770 mm (30.3 po)	360 kg (791.4 lb)
PACIFIC COAST	800 cc	765 mm (30.1 po)	260 kg (573 lb)
RC30	748 cc	785 mm (30.9 po)	185 kg (407.7 lb)
HAWK GT	647 cc	778 mm (30.6 po)	168 kg (370.3 lb)
CBR	598 cc	780 mm (30.7 po)	184 kg (405.5 lb)
CB-1	399 cc	770 mm (30.3 po)	166 kg (365.9 lb)
ELITE R	49 cc	735 mm (28.9 po)	57.5 kg (126.7 lb)
ELITE 50 ES	49 cc	730 mm (28.7 po)	49 kg (108 lb)
NX125	124 cc	805 mm (31.7 po)	113.5 kg (250.2 lb)
CR250R	249 cc	970 mm (38.2 po)	97 kg (213.8 lb)
CR125R	124.8 cc	945 mm (37 po)	87.5 kg (192.9 lb)
Z50R	49 cc	575 mm (22.6 po)	49.5 kg (109 lb)
FOURTRAX 300 4X4	282 cc	800 mm (31.5 po)	220 kg (484.9 lb)
FOURTRAX 300	282 cc	765 mm (30.1 po)	200 kg (440.8 lb)
TOUTES LES SPÉCIFICATIONS SONT SUJETTES À CHANGEMENT SANS PRÉAVIS.			

ÇA VAUT LA PEINE DE PARTIR AVEC HONDA. Honda et le concessionnaire Honda participant te rembourseront tes frais d'inscription à tout cours approuvé et complété de conduite d'une motocyclette si tu achètes une Honda neuve en 1989. L'offre est valable pour toutes les motocyclettes Honda légales pour la route de modèles 1988 et 1989 de 125 cc à 650 cc achetées en 1989. Le concessionnaire Honda te fournira tous les renseignements nécessaires.

C'EST BRILLANT D'ÊTRE PRUDENT. PORTE TOUJOURS UN CASQUE, DES LUNETTES DE SÉCURITÉ ET DES VÊTEMENTS PROTECTEURS APPROPRIÉS AU GUIDON DE TA MOTOCYCLETTE OU DE TON FOURTRAX HONDA. TON COMPORTEMENT AU GUIDON AFFECTE LA RÉPUTATION DE TOUS LES MOTOCYCLISTES. PAS D'ALCOOL AU GUIDON. SOIS UN SPÉCIALISTE. SUIS UN COURS DE CONDUITE APPROUVÉ PAR LE GOUVERNEMENT DU QUÉBEC OU UN COURS DE CONDUITE APPROUVÉ POUR LES VTT.

Right: First year for the Shasta White handlebars, 1989-1999. Shasta White front number plate 1988-1999. Only late model Z50R to have a red front fender. 1988, 1991-1999 all Shasta White.

Below: Red seat with Shasta White "Z" logos on each side and Shasta White "Honda on the rear of the seat. A one year seat design. A red rear tail with Shasta White number plates, 1988-1989.

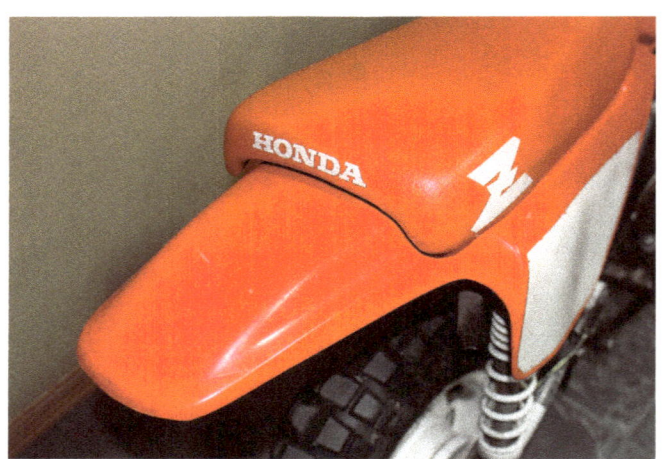

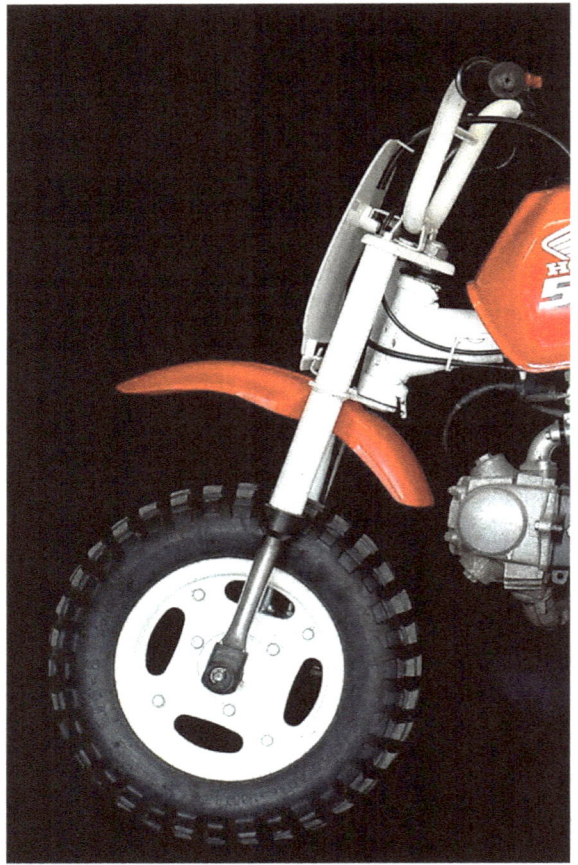

Chapter 23
1991 Z50R

Engine serial number beginning and ending: AB02E-6000001 - AB02E-6099999
Frame number beginning and ending: JH2AB020*MS000004 - JH2AB020*MS005474
Carburetor serial number: PA03F B

The 1990 model Z50Rs would prove to be very similar in style to the new design scheme of 1988-89. The most notable features would be the seat colors and logos, the tank graphics, engine cover colors, and the tail graphics.

The 1991 Mini Trail featured an all-white look that would last until the end of the Z50R production in 1999. The wheels, bars, rear tail, front fender, front number plate, and rear shocks were all Shasta White for the 1991-1999 Z50Rs.

All '91-'99 Z50Rs came with black hand grips, throttle cables, and front brake cables. They all had an aluminum front brake lever, with an aluminum bar mounted on/off kill switch, a black foot pedal with matching black kick start arm, shifter, and foot peg assembly. They all came with IRC Tractor Grip tires, and a black muffler with matching black upper and two-piece lower heat shields. The Mini Trail featured a Blaze Red seat for 1991 with a white brush stroke look with

Shasta White paint and plastics 1991-1999.

Blaze Red seat with brush stroked Shasta White "50R" and Rainbow Blue rear number plate decals.

"50R" present in the middle of the logo and a white Honda logo on the back of the seat.

The rear shock design remained the same as the '88-'89 models. The rear tail, like the rest of the mini trail, was Shasta White and it featured Rainbow Blue number plate side graphics. The rear fender had two warning labels on it for rider safety; the top decal being a larger label, which ran for the '91 and '92 models only. The '91 and all of the remaining Z50Rs would feature 49cc capacitor discharge (C.D.I.) ignitions with 3-speed automatic transmissions.

With the release of the new design, sales doubled from those of the late 1980s. In all, 5,471 units were sold for 1991 and the Z50R Mini Trail was revived. The redesigned Z50R for the 1990's set the tone for the next 9 years and sales would remain steady at around 4-5,000 units per year.

Rainbow Blue and Blaze Red tank decals.

IRC Tractor Grip tires, used on all 1988-1999 Z50Rs

1991-1992 exclusive 2-piece rear tail warning decal set.

Shasta White front number plate and front fender-1991-1999.

127

Chapter 24

1992 Z50R

Engine serial number beginning and ending: AB02E-6400001 - AB02E-6407025
Frame number beginning and ending: JH2AB020*NK100001 - JH2AB020*NK005410
Carburetor serial number: PH03M A

For 1992 the Mini Trail featured a Blaze Red seat with block-style wording featuring "50R" in white. This time the tank did not feature the Honda wing, but rather a large "Z" in Rainbow Blue, outlined in Blaze Red with the word Honda below it in Rainbow Blue.

The rear tail, just like the previous model, featured the Rainbow Blue number plate panels on each side with the two '91-'92 specific warning labels on the rear fender. All other components remained the same as the previous year.

In all, 5,410 units were sold in '92, just sixty-one fewer than the previous year. This was good news for Honda because it proved that sales were holding steady.

Featured here is a low hour 1992, currently owned by Chad Polson purchased from the Gregg Davidian collection in New Jersey.

Shasta White paint and plastics 1991-1999.

Aluminum on/off kill switch 1991-1999.

Blaze Red seat with block style "50R" logos in Shasta White.

Black exhaust 1988-1999.

Tank decal with a large "Z" in Rainbow Blue, outlined in Blaze Red with Honda in Rainbow Blue.

129

Chapter 25

1993 Z50R

Engine serial number beginning and ending: AB02E-6500001 - AB02E-6506519
Frame number beginning and ending: JH2AB020*PK200001 - Not Available
Carburetor serial number: PH03M A

The 1993 Mini Trail featured a Fluorescent Red seat with a large white block style "Honda" logo on each side and a white Honda logo on the back. There were also seats produced with the large Honda side graphics and no name on the rear of the seat.

The tank logo featured a large "Z" logo in Rainbow Blue outlined in Fluorescent Red with "50R" below it in Shasta White. The rear tail with its Rainbow Blue number plates, were the same as the two previous model years. Honda added a third warning decal for this model year. All other components were the same as the previous model year.

No production numbers have been reported for the '93 model year.

Rainbow Blue "Z" logo outlined in Fluorescent Red with "50R" below it in Shasta White. Two warning decals on the top of the rear tail, 1993 only. Note the all-new large white chain guard decal, 1993-1999.

Fluorescent Red seat with Shasta White Honda logo on each Side-Rainbow Blue number plate decals.

Black exhaust, shifter, pegs, and foot brake pedal 1988-1999.

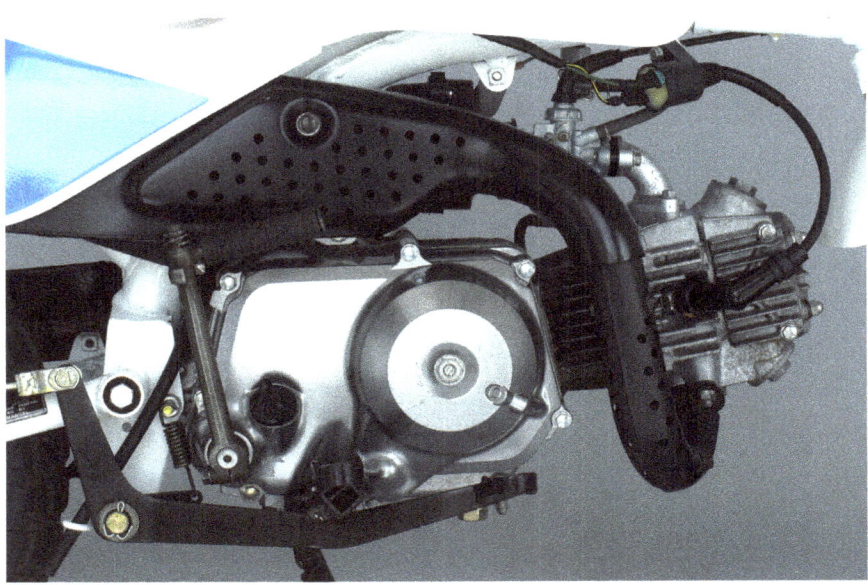

Chapter 26

1994 Z50R

Engine serial number beginning and ending: AB02E-6000001 - AB02E-6099999
Frame number beginning and ending: JH2AB020*RK300001 - JH2AB020*RK304687
Carburetor serial number: PA03M C

The 1994 Mini Trail featured a Fluorescent Red seat with a white paint brush style graphic that featured a "50R" logo in the center on each side and a white Honda logo on the back. This would be the last orange seat Honda would use on a Mini Trail.

The tank featured a large "Z" in Neo Blue, outlined in Fluorescent Red with the Honda wording also in Fluorescent Red. The rear tail featured a Neo Blue number plate to match the "Z" on the tank. It's interesting to note that this style number plate decal would only be used on this model year. All other components remained the same as the previous model year.

Production numbers are far higher than the internet posted 399 units manufactured. I know of a few '94 models, including one that Jerry Ure. Jr. owns in the 4,000 serial number range as well as one that my hometown friend Chris Langdon owns that is the 4,513th '94 produced. I believe that the 1994 production is similar to the rest of the 1990's production figures, somewhere in the 4,000 to just over 5,000 range.

Neo Blue side plate decals to match the tank. This is the only Z50R to feature the Neo Blue number plate decals. Brent Kolada Collection.

Fluorescent Red seat with Shasta White paint brush style "50R" graphics. 3-piece warning decal set on rear tail-1994-1999.

1994 Z50R brochure.

Chapter 27
1995 Z50R

Engine serial number beginning and ending: AB02E-6600001 - AB02E-6605419
Frame number beginning and ending: JH2AB020*SK400001 - JH2AB020*SK404958
Carburetor serial number: PA03M C

The 1995 Mini Trail featured an Atomic Red seat with a Shasta White "50R" logo on each side and a white Honda logo on the back. The tank featured a large "Z" in Atomic Red and white outlined in Uranus Violet with a matching Honda logo at the bottom.

The rear tail decals were switched from Neo Blue which was used on the previous model to Uranus Violet to match the new tank design. All other components remained the same as the previous model year.

Sales remained steady for 1994. In all, 4,958 Mini Trails were sold in 1995.

Shasta White front fender and front number plate. White chain guard decal 1993-1999. Z50R exclusive Honda "Made in Japan" flywheel cover-1991-1999. XR 50 covers do not have the "Made in Japan" verbiage and often times are found on restored Z50Rs.

Uranus Violet and Atomic Red decal on a Shasta White Tank.

Atomic red seat with white "50R" logo and Uranus Violet number plate decals.

Chapter 28

1996 Z50R

Engine serial number beginning and ending: AB02E-6605420 - AB02E-6610729
Frame number beginning and ending: JH2AB020*TK500001 - JH2AB020*TK504813
Carburetor serial number: PA03M C

The 1996 Mini Trail featured an Atomic Red seat with a white "50R" logo and a white Honda logo on the back. The tank sported a Shasta White "Z" outlined in Atomic Red. The "Z" is outlined by a Uranus Violet design with a Shasta White Honda logo below the "Z".

This was the last model that featured the rear tail decals; they matched the Uranus Violet tank decals and the look of the 1995 decals. The top of rear cowl featured three warning decals. The top decal warns against riding double and advises you to wear a helmet. The middle decal gives tire size

An unrestored example of a 1996 Z50R-Gregg Davidian Collection.

and pressure. The bottom decal advises against riding on highways. The mini trail was intended for off road use only. This three-piece rear cowl decal set was used on all 1994-1999 Z50rs. The upper chain guard came with a white chain adjustment notification decal. This decal was used on all 1993-1999 Z50rs. All other components remained the same as the previous model year.

Production topped out at 4,813 units.

Uranus Violet number plate decals. The last Z50R to feature number plate decals.

Black exhaust, pegs, kicker & foot brake 1988-1999

Atomic Red seat with white "50R" logo.

Chapter 29

1997 Z50R

Engine serial number beginning and ending: AB02E-6605420 - AB02E-6610729
Frame number beginning and ending: JH2AB020*VK600001 - JH2AB020*VK604319
Carburetor serial number: PA03M C

The 1997 Mini Trail featured an Atomic Red seat with a white "50R" logo and a Honda logo on the back. What many people don't realize is that the '97 seat is a carryover from the previous model year. The tank sported a Shasta White "Z" with an Atomic Red Honda logo going through the center of it. The "Z" was surrounded by Atomic Red and Black graphics. 1997 would be the first of three Z50R models that came without rear cowl number plate decals. Again, all components were identical to the previous year.

Sales were slightly down in 1997 from the previous two years and a total of 4,319 units were sold.

First model without number plate decals.

Black plastic chain guard and black metal lower chain guard 1983-1999.

Atomic Red & Black tank decal on Shasta white paint.

Atomic Red seat with Shasta White "50R" logo.

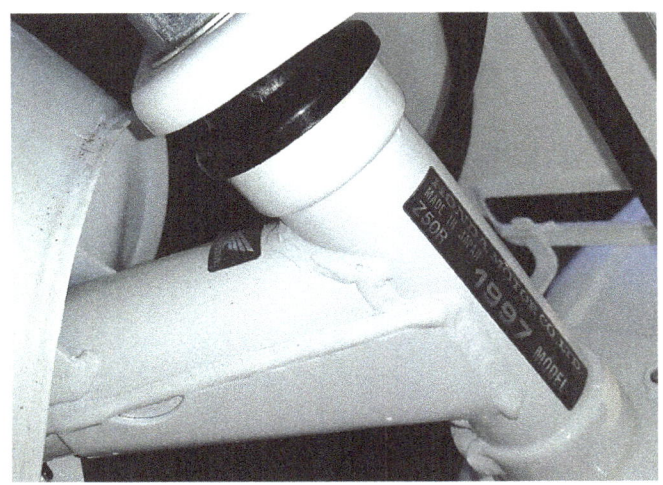
Top of Frame-Honda winged logo aluminum emblem glued to frame, not a sticker.

1997 Z50R Owner's Manual.

Chapter 30

1998 Z50R

Engine serial number beginning and ending: AB02E-6605420 - AB02E-6610729
Frame number beginning and ending: JH2AB020*WK700001 - JH2AB020*WK704964
Carburetor serial number: PA03M C

The 1998 Mini Trail featured an Atomic Red seat with a black "50R" logo on each side and a backside that closely resembled the backside with white logo of the previous year.

The tank brought back the old-school wing logo. One last time the tank sported a Honda wing. This time the Honda name was done in Endurance Yellow and it had a black "Z" below it outlined in Shasta White with an Atomic Red and black design bordering the center graphics. Like the '97 model, the rear tail on the '98 was without side graphics. The remaining components were the same as the previous 1990s models.

Production numbers for the '98 topped out at 4,964 units.

Pictured above: my brother Chad currently owns one the finest '98 Z50Rs on the planet. This Mini Trail is your stereotypical one-owner Mini Trail in pristine original condition with full paperwork.

Ignition coil used in conjunction with CDI, 1988-1999.

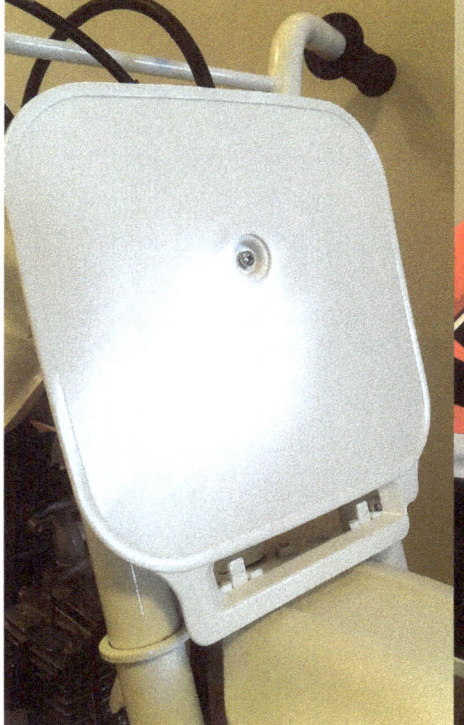

Shasta White front number plate, used 1988-1999

Final year for the famous Honda wing tank decal.

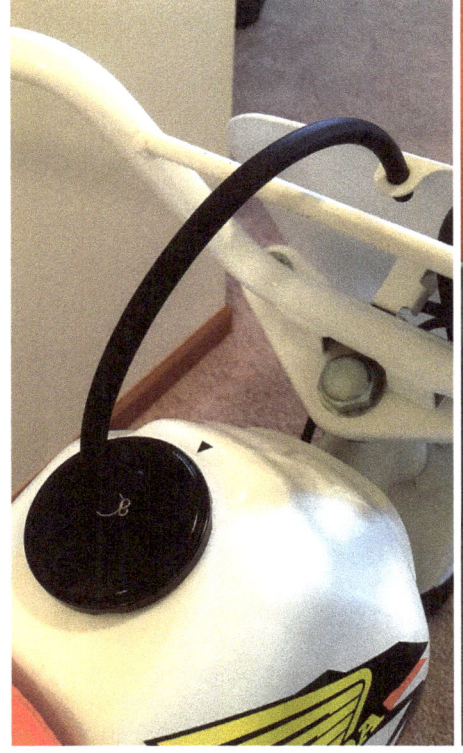

Black vented gas cap with tube, used 1988-1999.

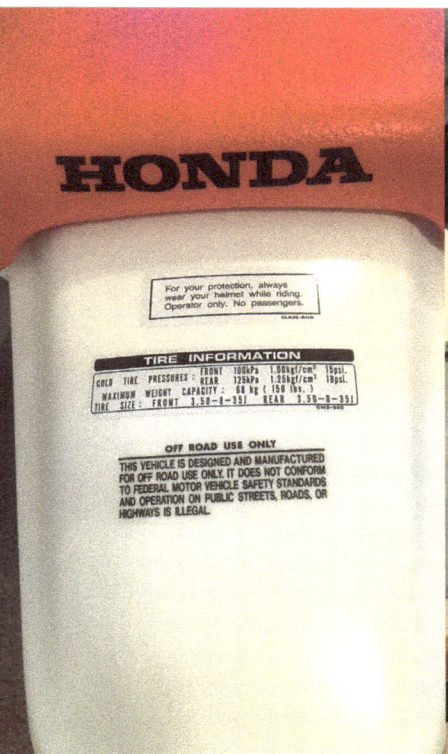

3-piece rear tail warning decal set, used 1994-1999.

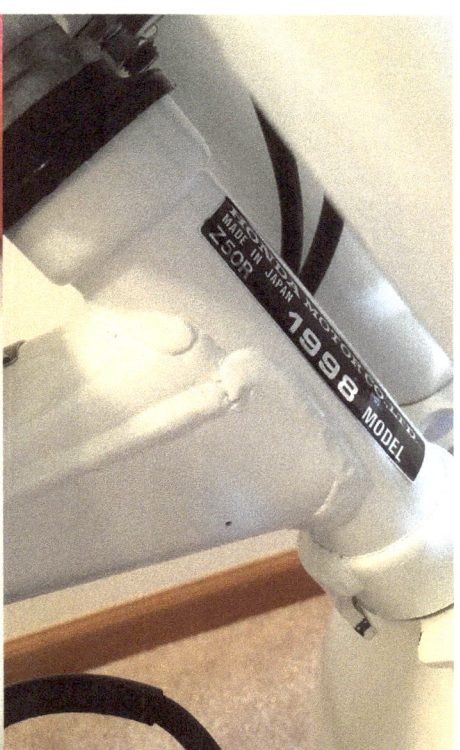

1998 Z50R black identification tag on Shasta White paint.

Chapter 31

1999 Z50R

Engine serial number beginning and ending: AB02E-6620650 - AB02E-9999999
Frame number beginning and ending: JH2AB020*XK800001 - Not Available
Carburetor serial number: PA03M C

The end of the line.

The 1999 was the last American Z50R Honda Mini Trail produced. It featured an Atomic Red seat with a black "50R" logo on each side and a black Honda logo on the back. The tank design was changed again for the final production year. The Honda wing logo appears in the background in Atomic Red with black pinstripes with the "Z" appearing in the foreground bordered in Shasta White. The Honda name appeared below the "Z" in Endurance Yellow. No rear tail number plate decals were present just like the previous two years. The remaining components on the bike remained the same as the previous year.

No production numbers have been posted for 1999, however there is a 1999 in my town that is serial number 5,066

Why:

You might be wondering why the Z50R line was dropped in 1999. The good news is it was not

dropped because sales were at an all-time low or because the interest was declining.

Honda decided to change directions and the Z50R line was switched over to an XR style dirt bike line to match the larger style bikes. The new version still carried on with the 49cc engine and most importantly, the Honda integrity. The XR 50 line ran from 2000-2003 before undergoing another change to the CRF 50. The CRF line ran from 2004 to at least the 2016 model year when this book was published.

Finding a 1990s Z50R is not very difficult. But finding a clean original version with an un-dented tank and un-ripped seat is just like the previous years, it continues to be a challenge.

One of the lowest-hour, 1999 Z50Rs is owned by my brother Chad. It is a French Canadian model and features front and rear blinker mounting tabs and French decals.

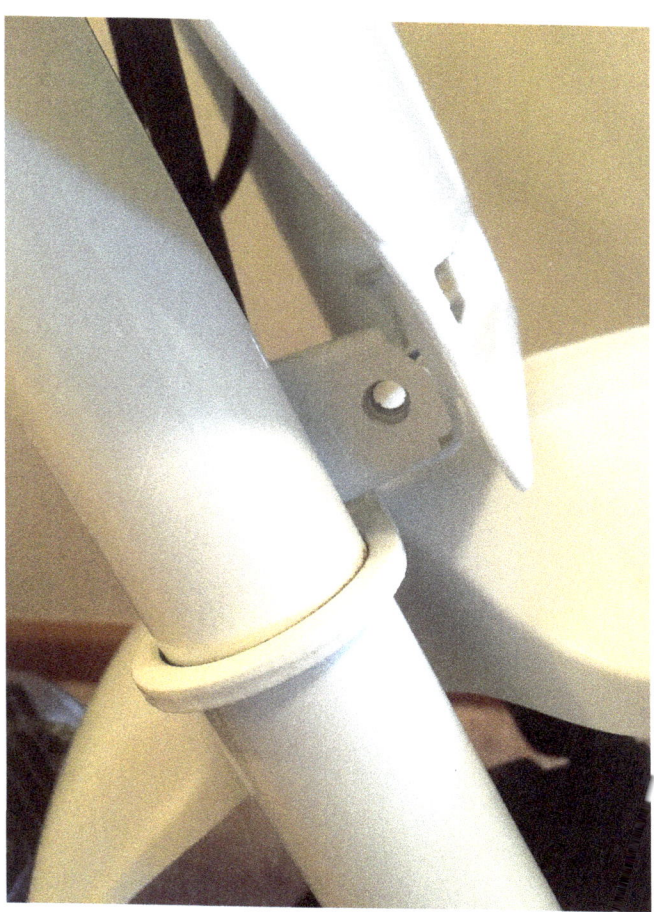

French Canadian front fork turn signal mounts.

A final note:

All fuel tanks, seats, and rear shocks for the 1991-1999 models have been discontinued. It is usually safe to say that when the main cosmetic parts go discontinued the motorcycle starts to become a collector's item.

Right around the time the Z50R line came to an end is right around the time that the Z50 as a whole started to take off in the restoration world and become a worldwide hit on internet sites for parts buying as well as online auction sales of parts and complete bikes.

The Internet made it possible for collectors to purchase parts and bikes that once seemed impossible to find. My brother and I looked for years for a back fender for a Z50 K2. We got to the point where we thought it would be impossible to find one so we left the bike as is. The first part we searched for on eBay was of course a rear fender.

Atomic Red seat with Black "50R" logo on each side.

Once the online internet sales took off, it changed the parts buying capabilities. My brother and I were some of the early pioneers for both buying and selling. The internet also shifted bikes and collections around the world as well. There are more Mini Trails in Europe than ever before because of internet sales.

For years, a large majority of the rarest bikes in the world resided in California. It makes sense with California's proximity to Japan and the state's population. Once the internet started to boom in the late 1990's many motorcycles started filtering across the country and often times around the world. Three of the rarest Mini Trails on the planet came to me from Mark Mitchell of Southern California. Each of those particular bikes spent its entire life in California.

Honda wing logo appears in the background in Atomic Red with Black pinstripes.

The interest level in the Honda Mini Trail is greater than ever. And like my Mini Trail friend Jerry Ure Jr. put it, "items like classic muscle cars and motorcycles that are collectible today will always be collectible. People aren't just going to all of sudden stop liking popular collectibles." I can't agree with Jerry more. I love it when I meet a Mini Trail enthusiast who is younger than me because the younger generation is what keeps the hobby going.

Here's to the next "50" years, and remember, "You meet the nicest people on a Honda".

French Canadian rear swing arm decal.

www.ingramcontent.com/pod-product-compliance
Lightning Source LLC
Chambersburg PA
CBHW041242240426
43668CB00025B/2463